FREE ENTERPRISE

A JUDEO-CHRISTIAN DEFENSE

HAROLD LINDSELL

TYNDALE HOUSE PUBLISHERS, INC.   WHEATON, ILLINOIS

All Bible quotations are from the King James
Version unless otherwise indicated.

Second printing, May 1983
Library of Congress Catalog Card Number 81-84289
ISBN 0-8423-0922-5, paper
Printed in the United States of America

CONTENTS

PREFACE

Scores of books have been written about socialism. Today the number of books which are critical of this philosophy have increased considerably. On the other hand, more and more books in support of socialism continue to flow from the pens of those who profess some sort of adherence to the Christian tradition.

The advocates of socialism within the church are often able propagandists whose success does not depend upon their ability to make a case for socialism. They speak to the heart, rather than to the head. In this fashion their support of a system which cannot succeed is most attractive to gullible students and bleeding heart sympathizers who are genuinely concerned for the poor of the world. Above all, socialism offers hope to the hopeless and its extravagant promises dazzle people who yearn for a better life than they have ever experienced.

In making a case against free enterprise or capitalism, its opponents employ the scapegoat technique. They delight to blame capitalism for whatever is wrong with society and for whatever evils exist anywhere. Since free enterprise is a complicated subject it is easy to make people believe what is not true and what cannot be demonstrated logically from the facts that are available. The bigger the lie the easier it appears to be to convince people about the superiority of the socialist cause. The advocates of socialism are often skillful propagandists who have learned how to use psychology to brainwash their victims. Many of them are dishonest in their methodology and consciously or unconsciously speak and act as though the end justifies the means.

Many of those who know the dangers and pitfalls of socialism can speak with authority about its economic fallacies and failures. But they rarely deal with this phenomenon with the propaganda perspective of the socialists in mind, or their use of psychology to mold and motivate people against free enterprise. Socialism has a great deal to do with economics, which has been dubbed "the dismal science." Scholarly works on this subject have demonstrated beyond a shadow of doubt what the innate contradictions of socialism are and what consequences flow from its economic views. Since the average man is not interested in economics as such, these scholarly books are not widely read, nor if they were, would they be easily understood. Generally such books speak to the head, not to the heart. And heart prejudices are among the least likely to be changed, for they are held passionately by people who are willing to make sacrifices to bring to pass what they believe to be right and true even though they may be mistaken.

Moreover socialism today is almost always tied into the philosophy of Marxism-Leninism. Anyone who has read the works of Marx and Lenin knows how difficult it is to understand them. And few indeed are those who are competent to respond to or refute what they read because they do not have the background knowledge essential for such refutation.

It is the purpose of this work to do several things which, hopefully, will help to keep the socialists from attaining their objectives. The first is to reach as many lay people as possible with the material contained in this book. The greater the number of people who understand the dangers inherent in socialism, the greater the possibility that this threat to national and international stability will be averted. Action should be based on knowledge, and knowledge should lead to action.

The second purpose of this book is to raise the level of concern to a point where the reader will determine to do something about socialism's drive to exterminate free enterprise. This constitutes an appeal to the heart as well as to the head. At stake is freedom understood in the broadest sense of that term, as opposed to slavery, which is everywhere experienced by those who languish under the yoke of socialism.

The third purpose is to make clear that free enterprise without the spiritual component common to the Judeo-Christian tradition is deficient even though it may still be better than socialism. The "human face" which free enterprise needs is altruism, which is simply another way of expressing the concept of neighbor love. No one can gainsay the fact that affluence may lead to a materialistic view of life which undercuts neighbor love and encourages greed. This is ultimately destructive of compassion and concern for one's neighbor. Contrary to what some have stated, a concern for the poor should be a motivating force toward free enterprise. And compassion for the underdeveloped nations should lie at the bottom of the drive to create wealth. For it is only by the creation of wealth that the material needs of the poor can be met and upward mobility achieved.

The fourth purpose of the book is to counter the arguments constantly heard about the depletion of natural resources, the ruination of the environment, and the need to defuse the propaganda favoring a return to the bucolic life of the farm (expressed in the phrase "small is beautiful"). Surely the environment should be preserved, natural resources should be used properly, and life should be made more beautiful. However, the threat of consumerism is not nearly so dangerous as the threat of starvation and the deprivation of several billion people. The West has been saddled lately with a neurotic guilt complex about its affluence that is not real guilt. The complex is built upon the idea that affluence itself is a sign of wrongdoing and the consequent condemnation of those who possess much of this world's goods.

In seeking to accomplish these goals I have tried to simplify the intricacies of economics, Marxism, the idea of freedom, and the reasons why Western civilization has come to its present state. I have kept the size of the book small so that it can be read quickly and easily. There is no part of the contents which could not be enlarged ten times or more to include data supportive of the propositions contained in these pages. I can only hope that whoever grasps the points I seek to make will go on from there to read some of the massive tomes which are available and which deal with these important matters in greater detail.

Above all I am concerned for my grandchildren. I want them to have the privilege of living in a country brought into being by a dozen generations of my free enterprise ancestors. On the maternal side, they came to America's shores more than three centuries ago. On the paternal side, my father was himself an immigrant less than a hundred years ago. All of my ancestors found this country to be the land of the free and the home of the brave. And may we keep it that way!

Harold Lindsell

INTRODUCTION

TODAY THE WHOLE WORLD IS ENGAGED IN A titanic struggle between two opposing forces: socialism and free enterprise. The struggle has been brought about by the advent of socialism into the economic, political, social, and religious realms of recent history. Free enterprise has existed among men since the days of the Old Testament. Socialism, under the badge of communism, is a recent emergent dating back only to 1917.

It is true that Plato, in his book titled *Republic*, conceived the best known of all Utopias, but nowhere in mankind's short history did any sizable segment of the peoples of the world actually bring into being a socialist society. In Plato's day men were keenly aware of the economic differences among men which at first glance seemed to have their origins in private property. This produced societies in which some men appeared to be masters and others servants. But the philosophical and religious systems looked upon all men as brothers. Thus there was a conflict between what *was*, as against the ideal of what *should be*. This apparently fundamental dichotomy has brought about the rise of socialism in the twentieth century, a system which seeks to destroy free enterprise, the only alternate viewpoint looked upon by socialists as the great enemy of all mankind.

Once we begin a discussion of the relative merits of free enterprise versus socialism, these terms must be defined. But first it is necessary to make clear that socialism usually takes one of two forms and each is the enemy of the other. The more important form of socialism is the one connected with the name of Karl Marx, and is generally spoken of as *communism* to distinguish it from utopian socialism, which may start with some Christian presuppositions. Both of these socialisms, as we shall see, have similar objectives. But they are built upon somewhat different foundations.

SOCIALISM DEFINED

In the broadest sense socialism is opposed to private ownership of the means of production. Thus all factories, whether large or small, will be owned by the community or nation. All farms will be communally owned as well. All merchandising agencies selling these goods will be also owned by the community. No individual will be allowed to operate as an independent producer of goods or dispenser of services.

In theory the entire community of people or the nation will make all decisions and work out all details concerning the economic operations of the socialist state. Nowhere in the world today is any socialist state able to operate on this basis, however. Therefore the decisions are always made by the elite, who in every case turn out to be those who have political and military control of the state.

Using the definition stated above, it is apparent that Marxism and utopian socialism share the same ultimate objective, i.e., the organization of society in such a way that the workers own, control, and operate everything cooperatively. The differences between them lie at another level. The first difference has to do with the method by which socialism hopes to eliminate free enterprise. It is the difference between ballots and bullets.

Marxism clearly states that force (if it cannot be accomplished by threats) must be used to destroy free enterprise. The use of force occurs at two levels. The first level of force involves the overthrow of the existing government and structures. Once the Marxists secure this control by force, the secondary use of force takes over. This means the elimination of the opposition, i.e., of the bourgeoisie, the capitalists, the imperialists, who are either killed or exiled to labor camps, where they are reeducated according to the Marxist viewpoint.

On the other hand, the utopian socialists hope to attain their objective by the use of ballots, not bullets. The aim is to bring about a peaceful reconstruction of society through the democratic process, whereby the people will vote out free enterprise and vote in socialism. In the doing of this they simply need a majority in control of the government, followed by whatever legislation is needed to bring about the change.

A second difference between utopian socialism and the Marxist brand relates to other presuppositions. Marxism is atheistic, is wedded to dialectical or historical materialism,[1] carries the notion of the class struggle to a high peak, and uses the doctrine of democratic centralism[2] to take away from the masses any semblance of control of the system. Whether utopian socialism could avoid the obvious evils of Marxism remains to be seen, for nowhere in the world is this form of socialism in control of any government.

In today's world the only form of socialism which offers a serious challenge to free enterprise is the Marxist variety. Thus, it is useless to concern ourselves with utopian socialism. At the same time it should be stated that any form of socialism, whether by bullets or by ballots, whether cast in a secular or supposedly Christian framework, has in it that which is antithetical to free enterprise—which alone can be validated by the Judeo-Christian tradition, as we shall see shortly.

FREE ENTERPRISE DEFINED

Free enterprise is based on the presupposition of the intrinsic right of people to the ownership, control, and use of private property. From this presupposition all other aspects of free enterprise are derived. Take away from free enterprise the inalienable right to the ownership of the means of production and it ceases to be a viable reality.

When we talk about the means of production we are thinking not only about goods which are produced for exchange or sale, but also about the other necessary parts of that process. We are talking about middlemen, whether wholesalers or shopkeepers, whether salesmen or truck drivers, whether bookkeepers or bill collectors. Farmers are free entrepreneurs too. They have the right to use their land to produce whatever crops they desire or to leave it uncultivated if they wish. They have the right to merchandise their crops any way they please. Free enterprise may be limited to individuals or it may involve employees who are paid by the owner (or owners) of the productive facilities.

Small shopkeepers as well as combines like General Motors, Sears Roebuck, or A.T.&T. are "capitalists." The man who buys an automobile and uses it as a taxicab is also a capitalist. So is the woman who owns a sewing machine on which she makes dresses for sale to her neighbors, to a retail outlet, or to some dress manufacturer.

Moreover, free enterprise carries with it the right of those who have goods or services for sale to set whatever price they wish for the sale of what they have to offer. Intrinsic to free enterprise is the operation of the market economy based on the notion that every transaction produces a result which is acceptable to the buyer *and* the seller. No one needs to pay more than he thinks any product or service is worth. And no producer of these goods or services needs to set a price lower than he thinks the buyer will pay. The seller will not sell for a lower price than satisfies him; and the buyer will not pay a greater price than he wishes to. Thus there is always a satisfied seller and a satisfied buyer.

A MIXED ECONOMY

Some people suppose that there is a third alternative to either socialism or free enterprise. They favor a mixed economy in which there is a measure of free enterprise and a measure of socialism. Usually those who advocate such a mixture think of community ownership of large industries such as steel, shipbuilding, coal mining, and the like. The socialism of which we are speaking here, the Marxist form, has no use whatever for such a combination. Marxists understand clearly that such a program will not, indeed, cannot work in practice. Moreover, it is quite incompatible with Marxist ideology, which is committed to the destruction of the bourgeoisie. Indeed Marxist socialism is designed to eradicate every vestige of free enterprise and regards even the slightest appearance of a bourgeois mentality to be a threat to socialism.

Curiously enough, free enterprise can and does allow for the existence of socialism within the larger context of full freedom or free enterprise. In the Western nations where free enterprise exists, any group of people are free to consolidate their resources and use them in a collective arrangement. In the United States in the nineteenth century a number of such collectives came into existence. The Oneida community, the Amana group, and others were free to operate within the boundaries of free enterprise. Their members surrendered their right to private ownership of property and operated on a communal arrangement. It was voluntary, not mandated, and no one was obligated to join. None of them is in existence today as a socialistic venture. But it can be said that their evolution from a socialist community to a more or less free enterprise operation was a consequence of the failure of socialism to work for a variety of reasons, about which more will be said later.

Socialism based on voluntarism is surely within the right of all who wish to live under this form of economic activity. But two important observations must be made. The first is that if private ownership is sacrosanct then no socialist state, whether controlled by a majority or a minority, has the *right* to take away the *right* of other people, whether greater or fewer in number, to pursue free enterprise as their choice. Secondly, socialism can never be considered merely in terms of economics. It is integrally related to one's total world and life view and penetrates political, social, and religious areas of life in such a way that it cannot be looked at by itself as though unrelated to these other important spheres of life.

No discussion of either socialism or free enterprise can leave out of consideration the most important element involved in any economic system—man. Man is the first, last, and the prime component of any system. In theory any and all systems have for their purpose the meeting of people's needs and the improvement of their human condition. The chief questions are which system performs better and what is there about man in his essence which makes one system preferable to another? This leads us naturally to a consideration of the nature of man.

THE NATURE OF MAN

However one chooses to look at man, the conclusion must be drawn that something is wrong with him as he is. What that something is differs according to one's world and life view. The Christian says that man has been alienated from God his Maker because of sin. Sin, in the Christian tradition, is the want of conformity to the expressly stated will of the Creator. The Marxist socialist takes an entirely different viewpoint about man and his nature. In what does the difference consist?

Marxism believes that the ultimate reality is matter, not Spirit or God. Thus there is no one against whom man can sin if the word "sin" can be used intelligibly at all. However, Marxism does allow that something is wrong with man. He is not rightly in tune with his environment and he needs to be changed. Thus communists speak about "the new man" that they are in the process of creating. The very use of this term makes clear that there is an "old man" and whatever that old man consists in is defective. In any event, Marxists do not say that man is fundamentally good. Nor can they show that they have yet produced one new man anywhere.

Of course there are those who think man is inherently good but has been spoiled by his environment. All that is needed is to change his environment and man will become in daily life what he is in principle—good. This secular view of man is dynamically related to the notion of evolution and looks for the perfection of man in the future through education, advancement of learning, and the like. In any case, there is no concrete evidence that progress has been made, and current trends suggest that man has been retrogressing rather than progressing. The crime statistics in the United States and the lowered moral and ethical standards of its culture allow for no optimism about progression toward the ideal.

Man's Basic Drives. People, both male and female, are motivated by three drives: the desire to be somebody; the desire to have something; and the desire to do something. Observing how people live will validate this observation. These basic drives can be used for good or for evil. The desires to have, to be, and to do are not evil in themselves. They may become evil, depending upon the motivation which lies behind the use of them.

The drive to be somebody can easily be misused and the end of it can lead to tragic consequences for the individual and others around him. Adolf Hitler had a yen to be somebody. He attained that objective when he became the chancellor of all Germany and then its dictator. This led to World War II with all of its deadly consequences. Millions of people lost their lives, nations were smashed, property was destroyed, and even those who survived felt the adverse impact of his actions for the remainder of their lives. He *was somebody.*

Everyone has the desire to possess things, whether money or goods. The quest for the material can be good or evil, depending on what the possessor intends to do with what he gains. Money can be used as a source of power to exercise control over the lives of one's family, one's associates or employees, or one's nation. Contrariwise, possessions can be used to alleviate poverty, bind up the wounds of the sick, and ease the pains of the underprivileged. John Wesley told his Methodists to earn as much as they could, save as much as they could, and give as much as they could.

The third great drive is to do something. This may be the desire to win fame and fortune as an athlete, an actor or actress, or a mountain climber who scales the heights of the Alps or the Himalayas. Some want to do exploits in politics, occupying the highest offices in the nation. Still others want to do great things for God—men such as Billy Graham or Dwight Lyman Moody of an earlier generation. What is important is not so much the doing of the exploits as the reasons which lie behind the desire to do them.

The nature of men and women is such that some will do what they do for the wrong reasons. Some others will gain wealth, do exploits, and attain positions of greatness for excellent reasons. They will live with what they are and do in great humility. But few are the people who are not greedy. Greed is part of the human makeup. Greater are the numbers of those sparked by greed than those who are motivated by altruism. Few indeed are those who labor for the good of all men without thought of reward or tribute.

Greed and human selfishness are part of the human given, constituting a weak link in the chain of life and conduct. Therefore the question must be asked which of the two systems, socialism or free enterprise, is more likely to prove beneficial to the greater number of people? In this regard free enterprise is far and away the better economic system to contain human greed. The reasons are simple enough to understand. Under free enterprise the people who purchase commodities are kings and queens of the marketplace. What they are willing to buy finally determines what will be produced and in what quantity and quality. Thus the success or failure of the purveyor of goods depends on his meeting the wants of the consumer in the best possible way and at the lowest cost. Since the purpose of free enterprise is to make money, i.e., create wealth, it is clear from the outset that the acquisition of wealth can only come about by serving the consumer.

Because people are what they are, the desire to better their material condition is never finally fulfilled. Once current needs are satisfied, new needs are developed and other wants come to the fore which wait to be met. If someone becomes wealthy by meeting the needs of others, he has rendered a valuable service to mankind and no one should begrudge him the fruits of *his* labor. Under socialism people are not free to have their needs met according to their own choices and decisions. What will be made and at what price it will be available is determined by the few for the many. The socialist consumer is never king or queen of the marketplace.

At this point it is important for us to note the attitude of the third world. The people of the underdeveloped world see what the people in the first world are enjoying, and they desire to have many of the same things. It is popular to argue that the wealthy nations are somehow responsible for the poverty of the third world. This is far from the truth. Third world people are *taught* to believe that free enterprise is the cause of their poverty. And they are also told that socialism will provide them with the things they want. Because they believe these views to be true, they naturally prefer the system they are told will supply them with what they want. Their problem rises from their ignorance and their envy. The very desire to *have*, of which we have spoken, leads them to envy *those* who have, when their own desires are not fulfilled. They do not *know* that socialism will improve their lot in life; they only believe it will, by a form of faith based on false information. There is nothing which the first world has that the third world could not have if the nations of this world were to adopt the free enterprise system.

A hundred years ago the Japanese people were faced with a situation not unlike that found in many parts of the third world. Japan is a startling illustration of a people who adopted the ways of the West, and by so doing rose to first class status as a wealthy or affluent nation. This is not to say that Japan, or the West for that matter, has adopted as part of the free enterprise system certain principles laid down in the Judeo-Christian world and life view.

Multinational corporations have also been accused of gross imperialism in the form of extracting large profits from underdeveloped countries, profits that really belong to the countries from which they have been extracted. This is another instance of misstatement of fact. Recent studies show that third world nations have benefited largely from the operations of multinational organizations. No one will deny that *some* multinational corporations have dealt unfairly with third world nations. But their record generally is good and the services they have rendered have met the economic needs of third world peoples. Their profits have not been outlandish. Indeed, third world nations would be helped even more if new corporations came into being to assist them in their quest for more material goods to meet third world demands.

The population explosion has abated somewhat, but even the most conservative estimates indicate that there will be six billion people on the planet earth by A.D. 2000. The vast majority of earth's additional inhabitants will be born in third world countries. They are the least able to sustain larger populations. Their economic viability *vis a vis* the affluent nations will decrease, and help from the first world appears to be a necessity. Only the free world with its free enterprise can help to provide what is needed to sustain the larger numbers of humanity.

There is no socialist country in the world which has maintained its food production at levels equal to what those nations produced before they turned to socialism. And the socialist nations are in no position to supply food for third world countries with their enlarging populations. The reason for this is simple enough. Farmers who once owned and operated their own lands, motivated by a basic desire to increase their wealth, increased their production. But when their farms were taken from them, the incentive for doing this was gone. Production lagged and declined seriously across the years.

The lesson is plain for all to see. When men and women are free, they will strive to be, to do, and to have. But when this possibility no longer exists, they sit on their hands. Until all the peoples of socialist countries become the "new men and women" socialism promises to produce, the situation will not improve. The only possibility for making the "new men and women" socialism so desperately needs is in some measure attainable by religion, namely the Christian faith, which socialism rules out and seeks to abolish from heart and mind. It is no wonder that the Judeo-Christian heritage is such a threat, for it proclaims the freedom of men from bondage. And human freedom has for its coordinate principle free enterprise, as we shall see shortly, when we discuss the inalienability of private property on which free enterprise stands or falls.

Man's Drift from a Religious Foundation. Western culture is a by-product of the Judeo-Christian faith. This tradition put God at the center of things. As Creator and Sustainer, God not only made what appears but he also laid down operating principles for the life of man. At the head of the list is the continuing relation of creature to Creator. Man is neither equal to, nor above his Creator. He is subordinate to the Creator. This subordination carries with it the necessity for man to walk in obedience to God's creation ordinances. It is precisely at this point that the failure of man has led to the current international crisis.

For several centuries, what historians have called the Enlightenment has been insinuating itself in the minds of men and has reached a position of ascendancy in this generation. The progress of the Enlightenment has led to man turning away from God either by enthroning himself on God's throne; or by coming to the conviction that God is dead; or at the very least by saying God is no longer significant in the life of man, who is on his own and can do as he pleases. The result of divorcing God from culture (and by culture we mean the economic, political, social, and religious sides of life) has been secularization. Indeed, what is appropriately called secular humanism is the polestar of modern culture, the point of reference from which man takes his bearings and toward which he points as he looks to the future.

When man works to be, to do, and to have, without reference to God, he falsifies the kind of free enterprise that has been associated historically with the Judeo-Christian tradition.

Free enterprise under God has always involved restraints. When the secular bias asserts itself, then the restraints which the creation ordinances had attached to free enterprise are diminished seriously and at last disappear. Socialism can exist in two forms: utopian socialism, which may have some Christian associations; and Marxist socialism, which is atheistic. So also free enterprise takes one of two forms: free enterprise under God or free enterprise under the umbrella of secularism. But there is a major difference between socialism of either sort and free enterprise. Socialism is at odds with the creation ordinances of God so that both forms fall under divine judgment. Both must fail as a consequence. Contrariwise, free enterprise under God will succeed, but free enterprise under a secular umbrella, because it frees itself from the restraints the Judeo-Christian tradition assigns to it, must fall short.

Today, what measure of free enterprise exists in the West is largely dominated by the secular humanism of this age. Those who attack free enterprise do not seem to understand that free enterprise has abdicated its historic commitment to the stewardship principle of the Judeo-Christian tradition. But they are aware of the shortcomings of a free enterprise system divorced from its true foundation, and they do not like what they see. They wish to destroy the "system" and replace it with socialism, which is worse, for it is under the judgment of God. It not only refuses to place itself under the restraints imposed by God, but it violates the basic premise which is foundational to the Judeo-Christian economic system as well. It repudiates the inalienable right to private property.

Whoever advances the claim that man has an inalienable right to private property also has the responsibility to make clear his objections to that form of free enterprise which is under the aegis of the secular. Under the impulse of the secular, free enterprise still is preferable to socialism, for its first premise about the right to private property is correct. But it is vulnerable to the charge of exploitation, injustice, and inhumanity when the restrictions placed on the free enterprise system in the Judeo-Christian tradition are abrogated.

Man's Drift into Egalitarianism or Equalitarianism. In the discussion of man, whose perfection will begin in the hereafter rather than in time, in the Judeo-Christian tradition, we must acknowledge the existence of two schools of thought with regard to man's relationship to man. Socialism generally is egalitarian or equalitarian. By this they mean that all men are equal and should be equal in all aspects of life, especially in economic matters. The inequality of man is the opposing school of thought.

The trend toward egalitarianism received great impetus from the French Revolution, in which the term "equality" was second only to liberty in the order of preference. Certainly there was nothing in the American Revolution which gave to that term the meaning applied to it in France or the definition it is given in contemporary revolutionary society. In American terms it meant the equality of man before his Creator. Outside of that, the equality the American colonists were talking about centered around life, liberty, and the pursuit of happiness. Surely it would be appropriate to talk about and promote the equality of opportunity. But it is incorrect both from a pragmatic viewpoint as well as from the perspective of the Judeo-Christian tradition to claim that equality can be or should be normative.

Men are not created equal with respect to gifts and talents. Sexual differences, for example, carry with them implications which profoundly affect men and women in their relationship one to another. These differences cannot be transcended. They are part of reality. Nothing is going to make women physically stronger than men. Nor can science enable men to become pregnant. Some people can sing; others can't. Some have business talents; others do not. Some have the ability to express themselves from a platform; others can hardly put together a complete sentence and have no charisma. Some people succeed in life; others fail. This aspect of life relates to man and his nature. There are some variables we can do nothing about.

Socialism has for one of its objectives the destruction of those differences among people, particularly in the areas of economic and material matters. All must be treated alike. It is on this plane that the redistribution of wealth has become commonplace in Western society in our day. The United States is currently committed to at least a partial equalitarianism in that it takes from the well-to-do and gives to the less fortunate. The progressive income tax is one of the devices used to accomplish this objective. When any nation begins a program of redistribution of wealth it is partway on the road to socialism.

Interestingly, the Soviet Union quickly discovered that economic equalitarianism does not work. Shortly after the revolution the notion of equality was postponed until communism at last replaced socialism. But until then the axiom "from each according to his ability, to each according to his need" was changed to, "from each according to his ability, to each according to his *work*." As a result of that change, Max Eastman, after he defected from Marxist socialism, wrote to demonstrate that the differences between the highest and lowest paid workers in the Soviet Union were greater than those between the highest and lowest paid workers in the United States.

The egalitarian view will be found today in many circles within the Christian churches around the world. Since egalitarian views are inconsistent with free enterprise but consistent with socialism, it should come as no surprise that some Jews and Christians regard free enterprise as unjust and call for its replacement by socialism. The depth of this conviction, and the frequency with which the attack on free enterprise (or, capitalism) is carried on, is frightening. It is especially ironic that the system which the Judeo-Christian tradition endorses should now be the system many people in the churches stigmatize and seek to destroy. Basic to the attack on free enterprise is the assault on the private ownership of the means of production.

THE CHURCHES AND SOCIALISM

There is no need to spell out in detail the attacks on free enterprise made by leading churchmen in places of influence and authority. But a few illustrations of this trend will be helpful.

Sigmund Freud, who was no advocate of either Judaism or Christianity, shrewdly observed that mankind had most to fear from the phenomenon of "illusion"—that is, "from beliefs molded by wishes" (Richard Wollheim, *Sigmund Freud*, Viking, 1971, p. 255). This is true of liberal optimism, especially of those in this category who are entrenched in the churches of our day. They repudiate or reinterpret the principles of the Judeo-Christian tradition to suit their wishes. They care little for facts or the verdict of history over the actions of men and nations.

Among the Roman Catholics the Latin, Gustavo Gutierrez, in his book *The Theology of Liberation*, argues passionately against the reformation of capitalism. He calls for its destruction and its replacement by socialism. He says the Church has been an accomplice in bringing people under the bondage of capitalism in the past. The Church "must place itself squarely within the process of revolution. . . . The Church's mission is defined practically and theoretically, pastorally and theologically in relation to this revolutionary process." The Church must be "for reform or revolution. Many

Christians have resolutely decided for the difficult path which leads to the latter" (p. 138).

Gutierrez argues that individuals are not to blame for sin. The capitalistic structures are the guilty ones. Therefore capitalism must be killed. And the socialism which he calls for to replace it needs no defense. It is simply the natural outcome of a revolutionary effort motivated by Christian love.

Robert McAfee Brown, then a professor at Union Theological Seminary in New York, quoted a Roman Catholic nun approvingly in his book *Theology in a New Key* (Philadelphia, Westminster Press, 1978, p. 179). She said:

The gospel mandates the poor to take what is theirs . . . no right of ownership supersedes human need . . . we know clearly that no matter who possesses food, it belongs to hungry people.

She said that private property is intrinsically sinful:

Repentance is directly associated with restoring goods to the poor. Sin, accordingly, must be associated with retaining goods that the poor need for their survival.

Moreover:

The Church is called upon to support the poor as they reach out to take what is rightfully theirs.

So spake Sister Marie Augusta Neal of the Roman Catholic Church.

Dorothee Soelle, founder of *Christians for Socialism*, was a visiting professor at Union Theological Seminary in New York. Her contribution included this statement: "We are at the beginning of a new chapter in Christian history. It will not be written without Karl Marx."

The United Methodist denomination is one of the most significant advocates of socialism. When it was still known as the Methodist Episcopal Church, its General

Conference in 1932 said that, "The present industrial order is unchristian, unethical, and anti-social."

The Methodist Federation for Social Action in its statement, "A Critical Study of Capitalism and the Christian Faith," said:

In keeping with the Federation commitment to replace the present struggle-for-profits system with a just and humane one, and in keeping with the biblical hope for a new creation, the study points toward the possibility for fundamental change in American social, economic, and political institutions . . . our hopes move in the direction of socialism . . . a socialism not defined by what exists elsewhere under this name so much as by the particular possibilities of the American situation (p. 1).

In February 20, 1979, the Religious News Service reported that Lord Donald Soper, the famed British Methodist preacher and former president of the denomination, "Sees self as a committed socialist." He said the labor strife in England made him "more than ever a committed socialist." He did not mention that the labor strife was a direct result of Marxist penetration into the labor unions and was part of their strategy to socialize Britain. Lord Soper castigated capitalism and laid the blame for all the ills of England on its shoulders.

Sojourners is a so-called evangelical religious magazine edited by Jim Wallis, who introduced a sort of communal community into the Washington headquarters of the operation. In the June 1980 issue of the magazine Wallis published his own article titled "Without a Vision the People Perish." This is what he wrote:

We are in a period of major social disintegration. The economy is rapidly being destroyed by the twin evils of unemployment and inflation. . . . Even our bodies show the consequences of a polluted environment as one out of every four of us now is afflicted with cancer, the plague of our technological age. Meanwhile, the number and suffering of the poor mount daily throughout the nation and the world, as a privileged few grow even richer. . . . The biblical doctrine of stewardship renders a clear judgment against any economic system based on ever-expanding growth and exploitation of the earth. . . . The power of a system is not finally in its wealth, military hardware, or technology. Its power is in the spiritual authority it has in people's lives. In other words, a system has power only to the extent that people believe in it. When people no longer believe the system is ultimate and permanent, the hope of change emerges. Undermining the belief in the system is therefore the first step toward defeating it.

Undermining America's belief in the free enterprise system is precisely what *Sojourners* is all about. The magazine has yet to articulate clearly what sort of system will replace the one it wishes to destroy; nor has it offered a powerful apologetic for the new system. What is apparent is that *Sojourners* favors socialism, for its earliest issues under the masthead of *The Post-American* were based on a Marxist view of the historical process with a thin veneer of the Christian faith covering it over.

The Episcopal Church produced a study and action guide titled *Struggling with the System, Probing Alternatives* (Washington, D.C., Church and Society Network, 1976). The study and action guide for the work said:

What we need today is not a liberal faith, but a radical one—a faith that takes us back to search for the roots. There are a growing number of Christians today who are beginning to define themselves as radicals—both theologically and politically . . . the truth of the matter is that one cannot expect to improve a system that is inherently irrational and unjust (p. 7).

The authors of the statement, of course, did not and cannot demonstrate adequately from either the Judeo-Christian tradition or the source from which it springs the charge that free enterprise is irrational and unjust. Nor can anyone do this without destroying the foundation on which the Judeo-Christian tradition rests, namely the Old and New Testaments. If the Testaments are not to be regarded as authoritative, then the opinions of the authors of this work become more authoritative than the writers of the Testaments on which the Episcopal Church purports to be founded. Why not then destroy the faith, as well as the economic system it advocates?

The penetration of socialist perspectives under the guise of the theology of liberation has also made gains among a few black theologians. A notable example of this may be seen in the statements of James H. Cone, who is on the faculty of Union Theological Seminary in New York City. Union has been noted for its left-wing radicalism and Professor Cone is no exception. It is important to realize, however, that he "admits that few other black theologians and black church leaders in this country agree with him" *(Los Angeles Times*, March 7, 1981, Part I, p. 32).

The *Times* reported that, "Cone said, he is convinced that some still-unrealized form of socialist democracy is the only answer to 'liberating' the poor, both in this country and abroad. 'I don't see how anyone can speak about liberation theology and be a supporter of capitalism,' Cone said in an interview, pointing to the profit motives of capitalists as inherently evil." He also said "socialism should not be rejected just because the Communist countries have not produced an acceptable model" *(ibid.)*.

Professor Cone appears to have no inkling of the fact that socialism requires profits for economic improvement. Thus if the profit motive is inherently evil as he says, it must also be evil under socialism. Any economic system which lacks profits is a dead-end street which would leave the poor still poorer.

In 1978 several hundred Roman Catholic and Protestant educators, social and political scientists, social activists, and theologians from North and South America met under the banner of an organization called *Theology of the Americas,* whose founder and executive director was Father Sergio Torres, an exiled Chilean priest. The conference issued a document titled: "New York '78: A Statement of Challenge," drafted by a committee comprising Dr. Robert McAfee Brown, a Presbyterian theologian then from Union Seminary in New York City; Joseph Holland, a Catholic theologian of the Center of Concern; Beverly Harrison, a Presbyterian theologian from Union Seminary; and Jean D. Rooney, former staff member of the Justice and Peace Commission of the Archdiocese of Detroit, of the Roman Catholic Church.

The nine-page document bore down on the evils of capitalism, which was called an "idol" and as such "a violation of the First Commandment for it demands human sacrifices to preserve the system." The document called for the usual radical change, namely socialism. Father Torres said, "We don't believe that capitalism is a system that harmonizes with Christian life." Torres, the former vicar general of the Diocese of Talca, Chile, "described *Theology of the Americas* as a network of Christians trying to produce an authentic theology of liberation for North America," that is, a theology devoted to the destruction of free enterprise and the enthronement of socialism, which is idealized.

Orlando Costas is another interesting example of the penetration of the socialist viewpoint into the minds of people who profess allegiance to the Judeo-Christian tradition. He is of Puerto Rican background and was raised in the United States. *The Other Side* magazine indicated he was at one time dean of the Biblical Seminary located in Costa Rica, a seminary begun under the auspices of the Latin America Mission. The magazine also said he was director of Evangelism in Depth for that same mission. The March-April 1976 issue of the *Latin America Evangelist*, the official publication of the mission, said he "coordinates the activities of the Latin American Evangelical Center for Pastoral Studies, including publications, pastors' retreats, and conferences." (The January-February 1981 issue of the same magazine says: "Orlando Costas, former LAM missionary, has been the head of and continues to serve on the board of the Latin American Center for Pastoral Studies, Costa Rica.") Obviously he was in a position of considerable influence in Latin America at that time. More recently he has assumed a professorship at the Eastern Baptist Theological Seminary in Philadelphia, Pennsylvania. This institution was brought into being to offset the theological liberalism which had so deeply penetrated what was then the Northern Baptist Convention.

Orlando Costas was interviewed by *The Other Side* (January-February 1976). In that interview Costas revealed how deeply committed he is to the principles of the Enlightenment and to socialism. He said:

I think it is the great shame of this country that after two hundred years it still has people who have to suffer real humiliation and have no freedom of choice. And it's because of the very system on which it was built. We still follow 1776. The electoral college is a good reminder that our democracy is an archaic system full of class residue. It is not an equalitarian society and was not supposed to be.

But the church has incorporated the American system into its own system of values and beliefs (p. 39).

Costas is correct that American democracy is not based on the equalitarian viewpoint. What he does not seem to understand is that the Old and New Testaments do not support equalitarianism, which is part and parcel of socialism—which neither Testament supports. The Church in America did not reject equalitarianism because of its willingness to subordinate itself to the political thinking of the founders of the American system. It rejected equalitarianism because it is rejected by the Old and New Testaments.

Professor Costas went on from equalitarianism to the acceptance of socialism, which was not in the minds of the founding fathers, nor is it to be found in the Judeo-Christian tradition. He said:

We who follow the Lord are led to a continuity with the poor, to a discontinuity with the powerful, to a vision of the cross in our situation, and that leads to socialism (p. 43).

He also said:

I believe that in the world today much of the oppression is the result of capitalists ripping off the poor, of capitalism stressing profits more than people. So I think capitalism needs to be replaced. But I am less sure of that than I am that oppression is wrong (pp. 42, 43).

Professor Costas' language is that of the theology of liberation, which in turn derives its basic viewpoint from Marxism. His antagonism toward free enterprise is deeply rooted in his psyche and not likely to be eradicated easily. He is against the reformation of capitalism and wants its destruction. He said:

Capitalism is not something that can be transformed and reformed. The very root of capitalism is the process of enslaving people, exploiting their resources. . . . The only alternative I know to capitalism is to reverse the whole thing and begin a proper distribution of the wealth. . . . We have read the ideology of capitalism into Scripture, and now we must rediscover Jubilee and all that meant in Israel. There we have the foundations, at least from the viewpoint of faith, of the socialist option (p. 30).

Here we have an illustration of a professing Christian who denies the tradition in which he was raised. He has deluded himself into supposing that his new understanding of the Old and New Testaments which supersedes the classical tradition is the correct one. This means that Western culture, which was built on the Judeo-Christian foundation and the Judeo-Christian faith itself, are both in error and always have been. Since the institution where he teaches was brought into being by capitalists' money and has always supported free enterprise, one might well ask the nagging question about the ethical morality of Costas, who is using capitalist resources to destroy the goose that lays the golden eggs.

One must also ask why an institution, built on a foundation which Professor Costas wishes to destroy, hired him in the first place. And the trustees of the institution should be searching their consciences, as should the administration which hired him. But the same question must be asked of all the churches who have on their payrolls those who think the way Costas thinks. So also, educational institutions, both public and private, which were created to sustain free enterprise as part of their rationale, must ask similar questions even though some of them no longer profess any adherence to the Judeo-Christian tradition. They are bound to the laws of nature, if not to nature's God, and this in itself should drive them to support free enterprise based on human freedom — which is lost wherever socialism gains control.

In the September 1, 1980, issue of *Forbes* magazine the editors carried on a dialogue with Paulo Evaristo Cardinal Arns, archbishop of Sao Paulo. The archbishop, in response to their questions, spoke of "savage capitalism." "The Church," he said, "criticizes the consequences of economic systems when they damage large segments of society." He called for improved social welfare and indirectly criticized Pope John Paul II when he said, "It's true that the workers, some of them, felt that the Pope stood aside from their cause when he preached against class struggle." The editors, in their introduction, acknowledged that in the Church in Brazil some "have been backing the incorporation of Marxist thought into the 'liberation theology' that has been spreading rapidly among Catholics over the past decade." The editors ended the article by observing that "Church radicals heap invective on a capitalist system on whose further development the welfare of their flock and the freedom of the Church depend."

The Religious News Service featured the pilgrimage of Cosmas Desmond, a former Franciscan priest from London, who spent time as a missionary in South Africa. He was under house arrest for four and a half years before leaving the priesthood, marrying, and turning socialist. In the book he wrote he prophesied that the Church in South Africa will die if it continues to support the capitalist system of South Africa. He said that imperialism is a contradiction of socialism and he wrote that South Africa's real problem is not racism *per se*, but capitalism exploiting racism with its consequent injustice and oppression of black by white. He argued that while Russia has imperialistic tendencies, it does not pursue them with the religious fervor of the moral crusader, as America does. So, for him, free enterprise must go.

In the October 1, 1976, issue of the *National Catholic Reporter* an article appeared titled *Vatican: Can Christian Marxists Remain Christian?* In the same issue another article titled *U.S. Marxists for Christ* appeared. In the August 10, 1976, issue of *The Washington Post* an article was devoted to Catholic socialists and their use of the theology of liberation as the starting point for their views.

Wherever one goes and whatever one reads about Roman Catholics, it appears that socialism is a live option and a favorite topic for discussion, books, articles, and propaganda. Apart from Catholic Poland, all of Western Europe has been deeply infiltrated by socialism among Catholics, and Latin America most of all. The United States has its share of Catholic hard-liners for socialism, or soft-liners who are closet socialists.

José Miguez-Bonino from the Argentine is a Methodist and one of the presidents of the World Council of Churches. He is a Protestant advocate of the theology of liberation.

In his book *Christians and Marxists, the Mutual Challenge to Revolution*, he says: "This book is written from the point of view of a person who confesses Jesus Christ as his Lord and Saviour" (p. 2). Then he speaks of his second presupposition:

A second presupposition belongs to the level of history: as a Latin American Christian I am convinced — with many other Latin Americans who have tried to understand the situation of our people and to place it in world perspective — that revolutionary action aimed at changing the basic economic, political, social and cultural structures and conditions of life is imperative today in the world. Ours is not a time for mere development but for basic and revolutionary change (which ought not to be equated necessarily with violence). The possibility for human life to remain human on our planet hangs on our ability to effect this change (pp. 7, 8).

Here is his third presupposition:

Still in another level lies the presupposition — which I shall try to argue throughout the book — that the socioanalytical tools, the historical horizon of interpretation, the insight into the dynamics of the social process and the revolutionary ethos and programme which Marxism has either received and appropriated for itself are, however corrected or reinterpreted, indispensable for revolutionary change (p. 8).

Bonino heartily endorsed a statement made by Juan Rosales:

He is an Argentine Marxist author who has given careful attention —and much incisive criticism —to the role of religion in our society. [Rosales] makes this rather startling assertion: "The bringing about of a true revolutionary transformation in our country . . . is for us [communists] inconceivable without the resolute participation of a renewed and engaged Christianity which is equipped to make its specific contribution to the revolutionary baggage" (p. 15).

Latin Americans and foreign observers are equally arrested by this new phenomenon: not a Christian-Marxist dialogue but a growing and overt common participation in a revolutionary project, the basic lines of which are undoubtedly based on a Marxist analysis (p. 16).

Two characteristics of this relation should be immediately underlined. The first is that the relationship is quite lucid and conscious —at least among the leading participants. The Puerto Rican professor of theology, Luis N. Rivera, quotes with approval the remark of the Italian Waldensian Mario Miegge: "I confess that I am a Christian, but I declare myself a Marxist." This position, adds Rivera, represents that of many Latin American Christians "who find in Marxism a language of liberation adequate to articulate their revolutionary intention." . . . "It should be inconceivable for progressive Christians" to envisage a revolution "without the orientating contribution of Marxism-Leninism or without the protagonistic activity of the working class" (p. 16).

Bonino goes on from there to endorse socialism (of the Marxist brand) and to damn capitalism. He dares to assert:

When we look at the history of socialist movements in this light some facts acquire a theological significance. While Asia continues to be visited by the apocalyptic horseman called hunger, communist China has practically eliminated malnutrition, illiteracy and premature mortality for 800 million people in less than thirty years. While the Caribbean countries, constantly "helped" by the USA, continue to stumble from economic crisis to economic crisis, frequently in the grip of terror, instability and inflation, the island of Cuba, subjected to economic blockade, has been able to develop in less than twenty years the basis of prosperous agriculture and cattle raising, has established universal education and is beginning to develop new forms of political participation of the people in public life (p. 88).

This blatantly false statement is not the end of the matter. Bonino's unadulterated endorsement of Marxism from the Christian perspective permeates the entire book. His heroes are communists such as Ernesto (Che) Guevara. He quotes from the writings of Ernst Bloch about the "red hero":

He confesses up to his death the cause for which he has lived and clearly, coldly, consciously, he advances toward the Nothingness in which he has learned to believe as a free spirit. His sacrifice is different from that of the ancient martyrs: these died almost without an exception with a prayer on their lips, confident that they had thus merited Heaven. . . . But the Communist hero, whether under the Tsars, under Hitler or under any other power, sacrifices himself without hope of resurrection. His Good Friday is not sweetened—much less absorbed—by any Easter Sunday in which he will personally return to life. The Heaven to which the martyrs raised their arms amidst flames and smoke, does not exist for the red materialist. And nevertheless he dies confessing a cause, and his superiority can only be compared with that of the very early Christians or of John the Baptist (pp. 135, 136).

Then Bonino draws this conclusion of his own:

Nobody who is acquainted with the tortures, the suffering, the death of thousands of communist revolutionaries —as we are today in Latin America —will want to retract or revitalize a single word of this moving homage. "Greater love has no man than this, that a man lay down his life for his friends" (John 15:13) (p. 136).

The story of the rise of socialism in the churches and in the ecumenical movement is worthy of a monograph by itself. What is stated here is only the tip of the iceberg. But the point is clear. Socialism which is antithetical to the Christian revelation, and the world and life view derived from the Judeo-Christian tradition, has established a beachhead in the churches and is gaining strength each day. Its adherents lay claim to the Christian faith but employ their peculiar thought patterns so as to wrest traditional teachings from their context. Despite some intimations to the contrary, the socialism of today is Marxist in orientation and cannot be divorced from that context. And Marxism and the Judeo-Christian faith are and ever must be antithetical.

Marxism is atheistic and its atheism pervades all of its thought life. This anti-religion standpoint is indivisible. If Marxism's atheism is not accepted its entire system falls to the ground. Thus those who try to use Marxism by substituting the Christian faith for its atheism do not know what they are doing, or they are deliberately deceiving the people they are trying to impress.

Marxism has a philosophy of history which is opposed

to the Judeo-Christian view of history. It embraces a theory of economics which runs counter to the tradition on which Western culture has been built. And it has a view of the state which is wholly in opposition to the Old and New Testaments. What is worst of all, the three major aims of this socialistic system include first of all the abolition of private property which is essential to economic sufficiency and to meet the economic needs of men. Second, it seeks the abolition of the family, as the briefest perusal of *The Communist Manifesto* will reveal. And third, it intends to abolish religion as well. There is no way that socialism can coexist with the Judeo-Christian faith. Either one or the other must perish.

CONCLUSION

It is against this background that we must pursue our case on which free enterprise is built. The next step is to deal with the central question of private ownership of property, and to this issue we now direct our attention.

[1]Dialectical materialism may be defined by dividing the term into two parts. By *materialism* the Marxist understands that the ultimate reality underlying all things is matter, not spirit. Only matter is eternal. Therefore there is no God. The *dialectic* derives from the philosopher G. W. F. Hegel, whose views influenced Marx. The dialectic has to do with the union of opposites. The process works through thesis, antithesis, and synthesis. The thesis affirms a proposition, and following this the opposing idea or antithesis comes into play. The synthesis takes what is true in both the thesis and the antithesis to form a new thesis. Every time this occurs we move one step closer to reality. The new thesis rising out of the old synthesis produces another antithesis and from the process a new synthesis is derived. In Marxist understanding we now live in the socialist age which will at last produce communism, which is the omega point beyond which nothing more can be expected.

[2]Democratic centralism is the term used to signify how a Marxist government is designed to function. In theory a "peoples' " democracy exists when the proletariat overthrow the bourgeoisie. But the ensuing democracy means only that the communist party, a small

minority, controls the government and makes all the decisions. The workers "vote" for whatever the party decides, and whoever fails to vote affirmatively is regarded as aberrant, that is, as thinking like a bourgeois person—and this is impermissible. The dictatorship of the proletariat turns out to be the dictatorship of the party or of the minority, and the centralization of power in the hands of the few makes all socialist regimes totalitarian.

THE RIGHT TO PRIVATE PROPERTY

LET US REMEMBER AS WE APPROACH THE question of private property that several options lie before us. Basically there are only two economic systems by which the world can conduct its business. The choice rests between socialism or free enterprise. It is true, of course, that some of the nations of the world have a mixed economy which combines some socialism and some free enterprise. Such an economy is characteristic of Britain and Sweden, where it is known as the welfare state. This sort of hybrid system is ultimately nonviable, for it violates the basic principles of both free enterprise and socialism, and cannot long survive the inevitable struggle for supremacy by these competing and antithetical ideologies.

Moreover, there are two kinds of socialism, one of which is correctly labeled "utopian," and represents a visionary ideal which goes back to the ancient Greeks. It comprises a human longing for a state of affairs which presupposes the possibility of an egalitarian society where perfection reigns and justice and brotherhood pervade the hearts of all men. This longing finds its expression in statements such as that advanced by Howard Zinn, professor of political science at Boston University. He wrote:

Let's hasten to say: I don't mean the "socialism" of Soviet Russia or any other repressive regime claiming to be socialist. Rather, a genuine socialism which not only distributes the wealth but maintains liberty.

That may not exist anywhere in its best form [nor has it ever existed except in the deluded imagination of some—my editorial comment], *but the idea has caught the imagination of many people in world history, famous and obscure, who were sensitive to poverty and injustice and wanted a truly democratic world society, without war, without hunger, without discrimination.*

There were Karl Marx and Rosa Luxemburg. Also, George Bernard Shaw, Helen Keller, Albert Einstein, W. E. B. DuBois. . . .

To break the hold of corporations over our food, our rent, our work, our lives—to produce things people need, and give everyone useful work to do and distribute the wealth of the country with approximate equality—whether you call it socialism or not, isn't it common sense? (Boston Globe, January 24, 1976).[1]

Implicit in the kind of world Professor Zinn so ardently desires is the usual egalitarian concept (i.e., the distribution of wealth with approximate equality), the production of things people need (i.e., not what people want, but surely decided by "masters" who think they know what people need), and giving everyone useful work to do (i.e., make them do what the "masters" assign them to do, whether they want to do it or not). At the same time Dr. Zinn will maintain liberty which turns out to be something quite different from what liberty has always meant (i.e., the freedom to do what one wants, to buy what one wants, and to improve one's condition above that of others by dint of hard work, saving, and provision for old age and for one's children).

The utopian brand of socialism advanced by Professor Zinn cannot succeed, and never has in the history of the world, because of the nature of man. Man is not fundamentally good, nor is he ever going to be in this present world. This was a compelling reason why Karl Marx, whom Professor Zinn idealizes, developed his theory of the class struggle in which he divided all men into one or the other of two categories (bourgeoisie or proletariat). In *The Communist Manifesto* Marx and Engels explicitly spelled out and answered the problem of man by dividing all people into these two opposing classes. They speak of "the clearest possible recognition of the hostile antogonism between bourgeoisie and proletariat" *(Capital, The Communist Manifesto and Other Writings,* by Karl Marx, N.Y., The Modern Library 1932, p. 354). Professor Zinn fails to perceive this fact, and it is precisely man's alienation from man which makes attainment impossible of the sort of socialist society he so naively advocates. Thus utopian socialism constitutes no compelling alternative either to the Marxist brand of socialism or to free enterprise. And Marx and modern Marxism in their traditional orientation speak scathingly of utopian socialism.

Marx and Engels in *The Manifesto* do clearly and correctly identify the focal point around which any discussion of socialism and free enterprise must center. They said: "The theory of the Communists may be summed up in the single sentence: Abolition of private property" *(ibid.,* p. 335). They also declared what measures were to be taken and what objectives carried out once they gained control of any nation. These are:

1. *Abolition of private property in land and application of all rents of land to public purposes.*
2. *A heavy and progressive or graduated income tax.*
3. *Abolition of all right of inheritance.*
4. *Confiscation of the property of all emigrants and rebels.*
5. *Centralization of credit in the hands of the State, by means of a national bank with State capital and an exclusive monopoly.*
6. *Centralization of the means of communication and transport in the hands of the State.*

7. *Extension of factories and instruments of production owned by the State; the bringing into cultivation of waste lands, and the improvement of the soil generally in accordance with a common plan.*
8. *Equal liability of all to labor. Establishment of industrial armies, especially for agriculture.*
9. *Combination of agriculture with manufacturing industries; gradual abolition of the distinction between town and country by a more equitable distribution of the population over the country.*
10. *Free education for all children in public schools. Abolition of children's factory labor in its present form. Combination of education with industrial production, etc.*

Elsewhere in *The Manifesto* Marx and Engels make clear that property ownership is signally important, and with this statement any advocates of free enterprise can agree. They said:

In short, the Communists everywhere support every revolutionary movement against the existing social and political order of things. In all these movements they bring to the front as the leading question in each, the property question, no matter what degree of development at the time (ibid., p. 355).

In order to accomplish socialism's objectives it is indeed necessary to put into effect a heavy progressive or graduated income tax which will destroy the middle class and wealthy. By abolishing the right to inheritance, socialism eliminates property rights at the death of the bourgeoisie, whose children will be left penniless. And by confiscating property, the system destroys the economic base for free enterprise of any sort. Thus we must assess the question of private property versus state ownership of property (i.e., the means of production) to determine which one is correct and which of the two will better serve the material needs of mankind.

THE SOURCE OF AUTHORITY

Once we are agreed that a choice must be made between free enterprise and socialism we are immediately faced with another problem. On what basis shall a decision favoring one or the other of the two systems be made? Stated another way we may ask: "Is there some transcendent authority to which we can appeal or are we shut up to the decisions of men who are of different minds on this question?"

Socialism (i.e., Marxism) is atheistic. It has neither God nor revelation to appeal to for a decision. Marx and Engels also refused to learn from the experience of the past. They said: "Communism abolishes all religion and all morality, instead of constituting them on a new basis; it therefore acts in contradiction to all past historical experience" (ibid., 341). But when we come to free enterprise as known and practiced in the Western world we quickly learn that it is derived from the Judeo-Christian tradition which, in turn, locates its authority in the Old and New Testaments. And the Old and New Testaments profess to have come from God himself. Now this authority may be rejected to be sure, but no one can deny that it was the determinative factor in the development of Western culture as we know it.

The case for free enterprise presented here is based on the authority of God mediated through his divine revelation to man in the Old and New Testaments and is binding upon all men everywhere. Because it comes from God it is normative, it will work, and it will prove itself to be superior to socialism, which can only be validated by denying what God has revealed and can only function by destroying the foundations on which Western culture has been built. What then is the case for private property?

A DEFINITION OF PROPERTY

Prior to presenting the case for private rather than public ownership of property we should offer a definition of what property consists in. Certain misconceptions require correction. Those who think of property as something external to man, consisting of only material possessions, have a very narrow view of property. There is much more to property than that.

Life itself constitutes property. Every man owns his own life. His body belongs to him in a unique way. Whoever therefore deprives anyone of his life has taken this form of property from him. But more than life itself is at stake. Free speech, free and peaceful assembly, religion and worship, as well as due process are property. John Locke, for example, correctly proclaimed that people have property in their persons as well as in their possessions.

To these properties we must add one which is, curiously enough, sacrosanct to those who so often are enemies of free enterprise, namely teachers in academia. Academic freedom is the magic lantern of socialists who demand the very freedom by which they seek to dismember free enterprise It is the free enterprise system which asserts that this freedom is a human right which cannot be abridged by anyone. Academic freedom is property, and consists first in the opinions one holds and the right to air those opinions publicly by oral and written means. Members of the academic community sell themselves and their ideas to institutions, and it is to be supposed that the salaries they receive constitute payment for something they have the right to sell. If they are paid for opinions they have no right to express (i.e., to sell) they are stealing!

Moreover, ideas are property too. Professors who write books to expound their ideas secure copyrights which protect their words against plagiarism. *Das Kapital* by Karl Marx was protected by copyright. Just try to find a new book published by a socialist which is not protected by a copyright! The simple truth is that socialists consistently violate their basic premise about private property in areas such as this so that they may profit from their labors!

Other illustrations of ideas as property abound. Men dream up new or different ways of doing things. Those of inventive mind have their ideas protected by patents. Do not new ways of doing things, or new ideas which have never been thought of before belong to their inventors? Surely if people have property rights in their ideas, then it follows that they must also be free to merchandise those ideas or even keep them to themselves as they please. Thus property begins with people themselves and the right to all things in themselves. This right then extends to those material possessions which lie outside of people as well. These properties are indivisible. Take away external property from people and internal property is the next and ultimate victim. Obversely, take from people their internal rights to property and their external rights wither on the vine.

Once property has been defined and understood, the next question which demands a verdict is this: "If there is such a thing as property, as we have described it, to whom does the property belong? Does it belong to the individual or to the community?" Asked another way, the pressing question is: "Is *private* property inalienable?"

THE INALIENABILITY OF PRIVATE PROPERTY

Our first claim is that private ownership of property belongs to the essence of life or reality. It is not something invented, devised, or conferred on men by other men. Like the law of gravity it is a given in nature by the creative fiat of nature's God. Property cannot be separated from economics; and economic matters, however much men may fail to perceive or understand them, are governed by economic laws. Socialism persistently flouts the laws of economics and does so because its basic presuppositions are opposed to these laws. Free enterprise *per se* is in accord with these laws, as we shall see, but when its practitioners violate its ground rules the system becomes unbalanced, and evils overtake it. Undiscerning or even well-intentioned people then seek to eliminate free enterprise and substitute in its place a socialism which produces far worse evils than can be found in some of the bad examples of free enterprise. They fail to see that reformation, not destruction, is the solution to the problem. Free enterprise is inherently good, not evil, but when its principles are not followed, evil results come about.

The right to private ownership of property means no less than that no one has the right to take it away from its owner. The right is such that no law passed by a majority or the unanimous consent of a legislature can expropriate property without stealing it from the owner of that property. In the Judeo-Christian tradition the Ten Commandments given to Moses were intended for the community of Israel, and for all nations for all time. "Thou shalt not steal" is one of the Ten Commandments. Karl Marx understood the true significance of this commandment. Thus he asserted that "thou shalt not steal" is the foundation stone of free enterprise or what he called capitalism, and constitutes a necessary rule of life for the maintaining of a bourgeois society.

In other words, "thou shalt not steal" validated and enforced the right to private property (see here *The Communist Manifesto*). It made that right imprescriptible or inalienable—i.e., nobody can take my property from me without stealing. That is why Marx and socialism (of any variety) must invalidate the Mosaic Law. Once they do away with the Decalogue and its God they can then seize property at will and claim the propriety of what they have done solely on the basis of their own dictum. When they do this they become judge and jury. However much they may deny it, they set up their own system of ethics and morality, which has for its centerpiece the abolition of private property. Their dictum in turn becomes an absolute. This dictum of socialism is clearly and intentionally incompatible with the Judeo-Christian world and life view.

We cannot leave the Marxist socialist dictum that private property ownership is wrong in effect without drawing attention to the socialist's own problem. Isn't it curious that socialism thinks it moral (i.e., that it isn't immoral) to take away the property of the bourgeoisie, in order to make it the property of the state, or, more loosely, the property of the proletariat, i.e., the people? Using the Soviet Union as a specific example, the new ethic makes its own commandment that it is somehow inappropriate for anyone to "steal" property from the state. The strictest laws prohibit stealing from the state, and guilty criminals are sent to Siberia to pay for their misdeeds. From whence then does socialism derive its opinion that stealing from the state is a culpable action, since they claim to "act in contradiction to all past historical experience"?

It does not take long for anyone to see that the socialist mentality is forced to adopt in principle what is contained in the Ten Commandments about stealing. But with this difference: The Mosaic commandment claims to have been given directly by God and thus is transcendental and has divine authority. But the socialist dictum comes from the pen of Karl Marx, whose credentials for being an authority in this field are suspect, if not patently ridiculous. The socialism of Marx approves of stealing when the property of the bourgeoisie is expropriated; it then disapproves of stealing when the property belongs to the state, even though the thief is technically one of the owners of the property which belongs to all. The socialist prohibition against the theft of state property rests on no enduring foundation and has a status which springs from the person of Karl Marx, who supplants God as the final authority. And in any society in which there is no room for absolutes, the absolute of Marx must also fall to the ground.

Once the proponents of free enterprise claim that the right to private property is inalienable, it remains to be demonstrated that this claim can be sustained from the Old and New Testaments. And this we will now do.

THE CASE FOR PRIVATE PROPERTY
FROM THE OLD AND NEW TESTAMENTS

Surely one of humanity's most interesting deliverances was that of Israel from slavery at the hands of the Egyptian Pharaoh centuries ago. The promise of that deliverance carried with it, by a covenant of God, the good news that the Israelites were to be given the land of Palestine as their possession forever. The prior premise, however, was that the whole earth belonged to God the Creator, who had the right and the power to give it to whom he willed. Thus the ultimate title belonged to the giver while the proximate ownership was held by the one to whom God gave the land. Moreover the land gift was in the form of a trusteeship which carried with it the responsibilities of stewardship for the use of the land.

When Israel entered the land of promise, all of the people from eleven of the twelve tribes were given a piece of land. The division of the land was made according to the size of each tribe, i.e., in proportion to its population. Special provision was made for the Levites, who were to be supported by the other tribes because of their special priestly duties. Each family got its just share, boundaries were set up, and the commandment was given that no one was to move the boundaries to steal land which belonged to his neighbor (see Deut. 19:14 and 27:17). The system was a capitalistic or free enterprise undertaking. Each family held title to the land it was given. Each family was responsible for creating wealth from the land. All had equal opportunity. But no guarantee was given that all would produce equal results. The poor were spoken of and provision was made for them, as we shall see. Clearly all landowners were on their own, and we quickly learn that some used what they had more advantageously than others. Indeed, some landholders became destitute for a variety of reasons.

The Jubilee law was established out of concern for those who were unsuccessful. The terms of that law are interesting. The plan was based on a fifty-year cycle. The Jubilee came every fifty years, at which time land that had been "sold" to someone else was returned to the original owner, debt free. The wisdom of this provision derived from the expectation that a fifty-year cycle would allow for one generation which had been unsuccessful to be succeeded by another generation which might accomplish what the previous generation had failed to do. It made possible a new start for the economic failures. But the Jubilee was not a scheme for the redistribution of wealth. No provision was made to take from some to give to others. There was no communal ownership of the means of production. The land, their means of production, was held in the hands of families, and could not be taken from them.

One of the key rules of the system was that no one could give up or sell the title to his land. In Leviticus it reads:

What a happy year it will be! In it you shall not sow, nor gather crops nor grapes; for it is a holy Year of Jubilee for you. That year your food shall be the volunteer crops that grow wild in the fields. Yes, during the Year of Jubilee everyone shall return home to his original family possession; if he has sold it, it shall be his again!

Because of this, if the land is sold or bought during the preceding forty-nine years, a fair price shall be arrived at by counting the number of years until the Jubilee. If the Jubilee is many years away, the price will be high; if few years, the price will be low; for what you are really doing is selling the number of crops the new owner will get from the land before it is returned to you (Lev. 25:11-16, TLB).

From this description, the amount of money involved when a landowner "sold" his property depended on the number of years until the Jubilee. The price was calculated on the number of harvests from the time of the "lease" until the Jubilee. But the seller who gave up the use of his land temporarily could not alienate himself from the title to it nor could he deprive his descendants of their inheritance. If the lessor died, the land went back to his descendants at the time of the Jubilee.

What the Jubilee did not do is as interesting as what it did do. A successful landowner who leased lands from improvident or unsuccessful farmers could accumulate wealth which was not part of the Jubilee law. If he had excess grain which he kept in his granaries it was not returnable. If he sold all the produce he did not consume, and stored away gold or silver instead of goods, he did not return any silver or gold—only land. There was no provision for a return of animals either. Thus, there was no redistribution of wealth, and neither socialism nor communism had any role in this arrangement. One farmer paid for the use of the land of another farmer for a limited span of time.

JESUS AND FREE ENTERPRISE

Immediately the question will be asked whether the New Testament did not supersede the Old Testament, and if there was some change in the economic arrangements to be gleaned from the teaching of Jesus. Both the statements of Jesus and the teaching of the apostles and other writers of the New Testament sustain the Old Testament teachings about free enterprise. And there are no exceptions to this.

Jesus has been acknowledged by virtually all men to have been one of the greatest men or the greatest man who ever lived. Thus even most of those who do not think him to be God agree that no one who ever lived was greater than Jesus. Did he change the teaching of the Old Testament and does his teaching reflect a bias favorable to socialism? The answer is no! And the evidences are available for all to see.

1. Jesus never revoked or invalidated the seventh commandment, "Thou shalt not steal." He reinforced it. When the rich young man asked Jesus what he must do to get to heaven, Jesus referred him to the Mosaic Law. he said, "Don't steal." When we recall that Karl Marx said that this commandment is the foundation on which capitalism or free enterprise rests, then Jesus was validating what Marx later repudiated. This means Marx was also repudiating Jesus.

2. Jesus gave his disciples the illustration of the tenant farmers in Mark 12:1-12, Matthew 21:33-46, and Luke 20:9-19. The story is simple enough. A landowner leased out his vineyard to tenant farmers when he moved to another place. He later sent servants to collect his share of the crops. The tenant farmers cheated him. So at last he sent his son whom they proceeded to kill. They said: "He will own the farm when his father dies. Come on, let's kill him — and then the farm will be ours!" Jesus plainly validated the right of the landlord to the ownership of his property and the right of his son to inherit it when his father died. He spoke of the judgment on the wicked tenant farmers and the re-leasing of the land by the owner to other tenants. Not a single word is spoken against private property as though the farmer owner had no intrinsic right to his property.

Moreover, if the owner had no inalienable right to his property then those who sought to take it from him were doing him no injustice. But if the landowner had no enduring title to his land, how could the thieves who intended to do him out of it have any enduring rights either? At last, whoever had the *might* to seize and hold the land would emerge the victor. Force then, rather than law and order, would prevail.

3. In the illustration of the workers in the harvest fields in Matthew 20:1-16 Jesus again validated private ownership. Here a farmer, "the owner of an estate," hired laborers to work in his field at harvest time. Some were hired early in the day and others in the late afternoon. The owner paid them all the same wages although some worked longer than the others. Those who worked longer argued that they had been cheated because they received the same wages. The thrust of Jesus' argument is obvious. The owner did what he wanted to do with his own wealth. If he chose to pay some workers more per hour than he paid others, that was his business. He violated no agreement. As the owner, he could contract with different laborers to pay them whatever was agreeable to the parties concerned. There is no socialism and no egalitarianism in these words of Jesus.

Here we need to be careful not to charge Jesus with injustice. First it may be that the latecomers equaled the production of the earlier laborers so that the unit cost of the labor was the same in each case. Also it is a market principle that laborers are free to work for whatever wages are acceptable to them and to those who employ them. Once they agree to the terms, only greed can cause them to protest against what they had agreed to in the first place. And if the earlier laborers were hired at the going wage they had no good reason to resent their fellow laborers or the farmer who paid them more than the going wage out of the generosity of his heart.

In the spiritual realm a sovereign God can give to the

repentant sinner, who comes to salvation only a few minutes before his death, the same reward that he gives to others who have worked a full lifetime for God. That is the nature of grace. For if anyone got what he deserved he would land in the lake of fire, lost and undone.

4. One of the most famous of all the illustrations spoken by Jesus is the one labeled the Prodigal Son (Luke 15:11-32). The younger son said to his father: "I want my share of your estate now instead of waiting until you die!" (Luke 15:12). His father gave him his share of the estate which he then spent frivolously. If Jesus did not hold the view that free enterprise is intrinsically proper he surely lost an obvious opportunity to correct the misunderstanding. Instead, the whole story leaves the listener or the reader with the distinct impression that Jesus did not challenge the father's right to his property, nor his right to leave it to his sons, nor the decision to give one son his share of his wealth before his death. And the father had every right, when he welcomed back his lost son, to assure the elder brother that what he had just done would not take from the elder brother his right to the remaining property upon his father's death.

For Jesus to tell a story, the details of which were incongruent with his views about property, is unthinkable and unreasonable. In other instances when Jesus' listeners misunderstood or misinterpreted the Old Testament, he corrected them. He used the dictum, "You say," followed by their understanding of the Old Testament, and then he added, "But I say," followed by his correction. That was the approach of Jesus in every other regard. But he did not do so here, and thus the story is fully supportive of the Old Testament approval of private property ownership by individuals.

5. In Jesus' illustration of the wealthy fool (Luke 12:13-21) he was asked by one man to command his brother to divide their father's estate with him. Jesus then used the illustration of the wealthy farmer who

decided to tear down his barns and build bigger ones to hold his harvest. But he died as soon as he finished dreaming and left everything behind. In telling the story with its moral, Jesus nowhere suggested that the farmer did not own his property or that he had no right to do as he chose. Indeed, Jesus told no story and set forth no teaching which can be advanced in favor of socialism or to support the idea that private property ownership is wrong. It is true that he laid down principles to govern the stewardship of one's possessions, but even this was an individual matter and was based on a voluntary response.

6. In still another illustration, St. Luke records Jesus' story about the nobleman and his ten assistants (19:11-27). *The Living Bible* speaks graphically about what happened. Before the nobleman left to go elsewhere to be crowned king, he gave each of ten servants approximately two thousand dollars to invest. Upon his return he called for an accounting and demanded to know what profit they had earned in the use of his money. One servant reported a gain of ten times the original amount and was praised by the nobleman. Another gained five times the original amount. One of the ten gained nothing. In fact, he lost money because he hid what had been given him, "Because," he said, "I was afraid [you would demand my profits], for you are a hard man to deal with, taking what isn't yours and even confiscating the crops that others plant." The nobleman responded by saying: "Why didn't you deposit the money in the bank so that I could at least get some interest on it?"

Jesus said nothing by way of indictment against the wealthy nobleman, nor did he suggest that he acquired his wealth illicitly. The only negative element in the story came from the lips of the imprudent servant who failed to invest the nobleman's assets fruitfully. And there is nothing said by Jesus to show that the servant's charges against the nobleman were true. Even if the charges were true, the nobleman was not responsible for what his servant did, nor would the servant's conduct be approved by God who is the final judge of the rightness or wrongness of one's conduct. The nobleman had the right to use the possessions God had given him as he chose, although in the doing of that he may have failed to use them as well as he might have. But Jesus' judgment is against the careless servant, not the wealthy nobleman.

THE APOSTLES AND FREE ENTERPRISE

The Gospels record the life and teachings of Jesus. When we get beyond the Gospels, what does the remainder of the New Testament tell us about socialism versus free enterprise? Perhaps the one incident mentioned in the Bible and the one most widely quoted to support socialism is the account of what happened in the early church as recorded in Acts 4:33-35. There we are told that all the believers were of one heart and mind, and no one felt that what he owned was his own; everyone was sharing.

And the apostles preached powerful sermons about the resurrection of the Lord Jesus, and there was warm fellowship among all the believers, and no poverty —for all who owned land or houses sold them and brought the money to the apostles to give to others in need (TLB).

No one can deny that the altruism of the early church was outstanding. Nor can anyone deny that what was stated as having occurred really took place. But it was purely optional. No one was required to do this.

The voluntary aspect of the illustration is what distinguishes it from socialism which is involuntary, whether the objective is attained by bullets or through the use of the ballot box. But what is most important to note in this instance is what happened in the sordid incident connected with Ananias and Sapphira, a story which is an integral part of the voluntary sharing, and what might possibly be called a sort of primitive communism.

Ananias sold some property. He brought part of the sale's price to the apostles, keeping back some of it while professing what he brought was the whole amount of the sale. He was struck dead for his lie to the Holy Spirit. His wife Sapphira came later and compounded her husband's crime by repeating his lie. She was an accomplice before, during, and after the fact. She also was punished by the death sentence. In recounting the case, Peter made a statement which thoroughly endorsed the right to private property and the right to keep or dispose of it, and to retain the selling price too if he wished to do so. Peter said: "The property was yours to sell or not, as you wished. And after selling it, it was yours to decide how much to give." Ananias was not obliged to sell the property. Nor did he have to give anything to the apostles, since the land belonged to him. The point remains that the property he sold and the money he gained by the sale were inalienable. No one had a right to take either from Ananias. This is the essence of free enterprise, even as Karl Marx and Friedrich Engels recognized. And it is the central issue which distinguishes socialism from free enterprise or entrepreneur capitalism.

One thing is certain. No one can find support for socialism in this section of the New Testament. The incident does exactly the opposite. It places the imprimatur of the apostles on free enterprise. This does not mean, of course, that people cannot get together on a voluntary basis to live in communal arrangements where no one owns anything as an individual—where property is held in common. But when people are forced into such an arrangement whether by bullets or ballots, it constitutes stealing and is forbidden by the Judeo-Christian tradition found in Scripture.

It is imperative to note that in the United States more

than a century ago a number of socialistic or communal societies came into existence. Not one of them exists today as a genuine socialist order. Human nature being what it is, these enterprises soon lost their distinctiveness. And the same is true for other similar experiments conducted around the globe. From a pragmatic perspective, socialism of this sort, voluntary in nature, has never made it. And we shall see later that involuntary socialism is not the better solution to man's economic dilemma.

In the New Testament the Apostle Paul wrote more about the relationship between servants and masters than anyone else. Nowhere in his letters does he indict wealth *per se*, nor does he place his stamp of approval on socialism. Rather his emphasis endorses the free enterprise mode of life. He laid down injunctions pertaining to the relations between husbands and wives, between children and their parents, and between servants and their masters. Overarching all of these relationships stands the law of love—"Thou shalt love thy neighbor as thyself." Paul said:

Servants, obey in all things your masters according to the flesh; not with eyeservice, as menpleasers; but in singleness of heart, fearing God: And whatsoever ye do, do it heartily, as to the Lord, and not unto men. . . . Masters, give unto your servants that which is just and equal; knowing that ye also have a Master in heaven (Col. 3:22—4:1).

Paul also wrote to the church members at Ephesus about these relationships. Again he urged servants to obey their masters and to perform their services willingly as to God himself. He commanded masters to forbear threatening, and told them to treat their servants in a way acceptable to God. He recognized the God-given differences which exist among men and which result in some being masters and others servants. Indeed, even with respect to slavery, Christian slaves and Christian slaveholders were enjoined to act responsibly under the law of love. Those who were property owners were not criticized, nor were they commanded or encouraged to establish an egalitarian society, which is everywhere militated against in Scripture.

The harshest words in the New Testament were spoken by James, who lashed out against the *misuse* of wealth, not the simple possession of it. His words do not apply to those who used their wealth and station in life wisely and well. He said:

Look here, you rich men, now is the time to cry and groan with anguished grief because of all the terrible troubles ahead of you. Your wealth is even now rotting away, and your fine clothes are becoming mere moth-eaten rags. The value of your gold and silver is dropping fast, yet it will stand as evidence against you, and eat your flesh like fire. That is what you have stored up for yourselves, to receive on that coming day of judgment. For listen! Hear the cries of the field workers whom you have cheated of their pay. Their cries have reached the Lord of Hosts.

You have spent your years here on earth having fun, satisfying your every whim, and now your fat hearts are ready for the slaughter. You have condemned and killed good men who had no power to defend themselves against you (James 5:1-6, TLB).

James roundly condemned the practice of wealthy people who unjustly underpaid their workers, and thus violated the law of love. In other words, free enterprise in both the Old and New Testaments included stewardship regulations with altruism a basic precept. Fair wages, as we shall see, are related to a number of factors which make for great diversity. But egalitarianism is never advocated and wages are related to productivity and to the economic laws of the marketplace. We must insist therefore that the laws of economics, which are writ large in the affairs of men by way of natural revelation, must be studied and understood and fairly related to wages paid to workers.

The Apostle Paul taught that men are gifted by God and these gifts vary greatly. People are to use whatever gifts God has given them properly and responsibly. He said:

God has given each of us the ability to do certain things well. So if God has given you the ability to prophesy, then prophesy whenever you can — as often as your faith is strong enough to receive a message from God. If your gift is that of serving others, serve them well. If you are a teacher, do a good job of teaching. If you are a preacher, see to it that your sermons are strong and helpful. If God has given you money, be generous in helping others with it. If God has given you administrative ability and put you in charge of the work of others, take the responsibility seriously. Those who offer comfort to the sorrowing should do so with Christian cheer.

Don't just pretend that you love others: really love them. Hate what is wrong. Stand on the side of the good. Love each other with brotherly affection and take delight in honoring each other. Never be lazy in your work but serve the Lord enthusiastically.

Be glad for all God is planning for you. Be patient in trouble, and prayerful always. When God's children are in need, you be the one to help them out. And get into the habit of inviting guests home for dinner or, if they need lodging, for the night (Romans 12:6-13, TLB).

Everywhere in the Old and New Testaments men and women are told to be productive, and God promises to bless those who labor as they walk obediently. Those who refuse to work are not to eat. This stricture does not refer to those who are incapacitated, or to widows and orphans. But it does mean that those who are capable of working are not to be excused when they fail to do so.

Free enterprise is supported in the Old and New Testaments. This is so despite the effort of some socialist advocates who seriously endeavor to prove the exact opposite. For example, Peter Davids in an article published in the *Post-American* (now known as *Sojourners)* and reprinted in the *Latin America Evangelist*, said that the system set up by God for Israel in the Old Testament was "a type of theocratic socialism." He further argued that the law of Jubilee which brought back to the original owners any land which had been "sold" or leased until the fifty year period ended meant "there could be no accumulation of capital" *(Latin America Evangelist*, March-April 1976, p. 2). Both of these statements are incorrect. Land or property ownership as we have seen from the socialist viewpoint is the key point. Wherever there is private land ownership, free enterprise or capitalism is at work. Thus the Old Testament provision for land ownership was not theocratic socialism by the wildest stretch of one's imagination. To speak of God's ultimate ownership of the land as though that would make for socialism is ridiculous. And to use the phrase "theocratic socialism" is non-sense.

Even worse is the statement about the return of land sold or leased for the period up to the year of the Jubilee. To say "there could be no accumulation of capital" is so naive as to boggle the imagination. Gold, silver, animals, etc., also constitute capital. So do ideas, inventions, and the like. There was no provision whatever for sharing this kind of wealth in the year of Jubilee. Thus there was capital accumulation dependent upon the business skill, acumen, life style, and saving habits of each individual.

What is more interesting is the question, "How did the poor become poor?" When the land had been distributed each family started with approximately the same amount of capital. But they did not enjoy the same gifts and endowments. All had equality of opportunity but that is all each had. From that point onward, how the people fared depended on their own efforts and the management of their affairs. Obviously farmers who leased or "sold" their land did so because they were not as successful as the landowners to whom they leased their lands until the Jubilee.

Furthermore, it is clear that some opted to become indentured servants to those who had succeeded in their use of the land. Provision was made for indentured Israelites to be held in bondage for no more than six years. Every seventh year these people were freed. But there was an exception even to this. For one who wished to continue in this relationship, provision was made to do so, according to Exodus 21:3-6.

The free enterprise system of the Old Testament did have some controls. Previously we said there is a free enterprise viewpoint which goes back to the Enlightenment, even as socialism does, which makes private property an absolute without any controls whatever except the laws of the marketplace. Socialism, contrariwise, has controls without room for free enterprise. The Milton Friedman type of free enterprise has all freedom and no adequate controls. The Old Testament form of economic freedom took into account the sinful nature of man and placed some controls on economic activity. Basically the controls called for altruism as an indispensable component of free enterprise. The year of Jubilee in which leased land was returned to the owners was altruistic. The release of slaves every seventh year followed the same pattern. In addition the land was to lie fallow every seventh year and whatever grew by itself that year was for the use of the poor and for animals. The same held true for vineyards and olive groves. Some ignorantly have supposed that work stopped every seventh year. This was not so. Obviously a process of rotation was practiced so that only one seventh of the arable land was left unused at any given time.

Moreover, a poor tax was instituted, a tax which in the case of Israel included support for the priesthood. According to Deuteronomy 14:28, 29 (TLB) the procedure to be followed was this:

Every third year you are to use your entire tithe for local welfare programs: Give it to the Levites who have no inheritance among you, or to foreigners, or to widows and orphans within your city, so that they can eat and be satisfied; and then Jehovah your God will bless you and your work (Deut. 14:28, 29).

In addition to these regulations, debts were forgiven; i.e., the debts were written off every seven years. Interest was exacted from strangers for loans but not from Israelites. Also the gleanings of the harvest were left for the poor, the orphans, and the widows. This has been beautifully pictured for us in the book of Ruth in the Old Testament.

THE MANDATE TO CREATE WEALTH

Throughout the Old and New Testaments the writers proclaimed that it was the intention of God for all people to enjoy his creation. Plentiful provision was made for people to use what God has created. What is called the "creation mandate" was a charge to all human life to create wealth. In Genesis 1:26-31 this mandate appears.

Then God said, "Let us make a man — someone like ourselves, to be the master of all life upon the earth and in the skies and in the seas." So God made man like his Maker. Like God did God make man; man and maid did he make them. And God blessed them and told them, "Multiply and fill the earth and subdue it; you are masters of the fish and birds and all the animals. And look! I have given you the seed-bearing plants throughout the earth, and all the fruit trees for your food. And I've given all the grass and plants to the animals and birds for their food." Then God looked over all that he had made, and it was excellent in every way. This ended the sixth day (Gen. 1:26-31, TLB).

The command, "Be fruitful, and multiply, and replenish the earth, and subdue it" has never been abrogated. It remains for people everywhere to do so, to this day. The New Testament also includes the many promises of God to bless those who heed his commandments and who obey him. God gave the earth and all of its fullness to mankind for their use as stewards. Any failure to *use* what God has provided is no less wrong than the *misuse* of God's creation. Within the boundaries set by God, people were free and are free today to do as they please. The innate desire to be something, do something, and have something, afforded for all a wide open door of opportunity to create wealth for the glory of the Creator. Mankind was free.

By creating wealth we mean that people produce more than they consume. If a farmer produces five thousand bushels of wheat but only consumes forty-five hundred bushels, he has an excess of five hundred bushels. This is wealth, for the farmer is worth more than he was the year before. If he sells the five hundred bushels for paper money (which is only a medium of exchange and has no intrinsic value unless it is something that all men want—such as silver, gold, etc.) he can use that money for a variety of purposes. He can buy more land to produce more wheat. He can improve his home. He can obtain more clothes. He can buy more books, etc. Or he can bank it and draw interest. But if he consumes all that he produces he cannot improve his economic situation.

Adam Smith in *The Wealth of Nations* correctly said, "Consumption is the sole end and purpose of all production" *(The Freeman,* July 1976, p. 404). It might be put this way: Why make dresses that will never be worn? Why grow wheat which will never be eaten? Why make baseball bats that will never be used to hit balls? The fundamental fact is this: All production is based on the desires and demands of people for things they want. Humans have an insatiable desire to improve their material well-being. Free enterprise is the vehicle whereby the never-ending race to supply the ever-increasing wants of man goes on. And enterprising men can create demand.

Thomas Edison invented the electric bulb. This created a demand by people who wanted electric light rather than gas light. E. F. Schumacher wrote a book *Small is Beautiful.* In this book he argues for a simple life style, the slowing up of consumption, and a return to a bucolic life along agrarian lines. Whether this is the true ideal for mankind is beside the point. Free people can choose to accept or reject what he calls for, but he cannot make them do what he wants because he thinks the way he does. It is not at all likely that what Schumacher opts for will become commonplace. The fact is that what the third world, poverty-stricken nations want is a standard of living comparable to what the industrialized West enjoys. Their desire for an ever higher level of material well-being remains to be met, but the desire will not be quenched. All people always want more than they presently have.

The common people today in many ways live better than monarchs lived a thousand years ago. And these people want to live better tomorrow. One might interject the fact that simply to make available to third world people what the West now has is a task of considerable proportions. To improve the well-being of the West at the same time will tax the gifts and abilities of all.

Persuasive arguments can be presented to prove that many of the items wanted by people are hardly essential to life. After all, we do not need fifty kinds of perfume, thirty kinds of deodorant, a hundred different shoe styles, more than one style of automobile, not to mention the necessity for marbles, cards, curlers, or the thousands of knicknacks sold every day in department stores. This answer is plain enough. These are things people want. People who are free, are free to want what others may or may not care for. And anyone who is free can produce and sell what these people want, or refrain from doing so. The only way the situation can be changed is to take away people's freedom and give them what their masters think they need and ought to have, not what they want.

Moreover, the creation, production, and sale of new items never known before is the right of free people everywhere. Creating a demand for a new product, which some may judge to be needless, is every person's right so long as freedom is not lost. Freedom does carry with it great risks. This is what freedom is all about. But these risks cannot be avoided without the loss of freedom. When freedom is gone, however, the risks of freedom disappear, but people are always dehumanized and denigrated when they cease to be free. Thus the loss of freedom entails paying a much higher price than facing the risks which freedom brings.

In creating wealth, free men take risks on their own. Society does not owe them a living. Their endeavors may succeed or they may fail miserably. If they produce items nobody wants or will buy, they are in trouble. The purpose of creating wealth is to produce something people will want, or to provide a service they will pay for. Sometimes all that a man can offer by way of providing a service is his own labor. How then can he create wealth for himself? He can do so only by spending less than he earns, and saving the remainder. That constitutes his wealth. He can use his surplus to increase his wealth further by a variety of means. He can put it in a bank at interest, or invest it in stocks which may appreciate as well as pay dividends. He can gradually accumulate money to start his own business, even if it is on a very small scale. Whoever spends more than he earns does not create wealth. He goes into debt. And no one can do that unless some kind soul lends him something with which to do so. There is always a pay day, however, and the debtor reaches a point, sooner or later, when he must pay the piper whether by going to jail, going bankrupt, or undergoing servitude to repay what he has borrowed.

In socialism no one creates wealth for himself. He can assist the state in increasing its wealth, but the egalitarian emphasis is a dead end street for the ambitious. The one who produces more than his fellow worker is no better off than the slowest and least productive member of society. And if all members of society are rewarded equally for whatever work they perform, who will exert the effort to master the most difficult and demanding jobs (when they can do menial work for the same wages)? Wherever socialism discriminates among workers and pays some higher wages than others, it is the clearest indicator that socialism has failed and to some degree private capitalism rather than state capitalism has taken over. When this happens the egalitarian principle has been sacrificed in practice if not in theory.

Socialism today offers the excuse that wage differentials are necessary for an interim period until the "new man" comes into being. The new man which it hopes to create is one of socialism's fondest and most fraudulent myths. Whoever believes it is either overly credulous or promotes the claim with an eye to improving his own situation at the expense of his fellow workers. Certainly, history affords no instance in which the new man has come into being, and there is no society anywhere populated by that kind of person. History, on the other hand, offers the most convincing evidence that man is not intrinsically good, nor is he inclined toward goodness. He is not born good and then corrupted by society, despite the opinion of John Locke to that effect. And for society to try to turn people around contrary to the nature of the society is preposterous. Only God can do that.

Free enterprise recognizes man's self-interest (a quality which, when balanced by altruism is not illegitimate) and uses it for the good of the many. He who becomes wealthy by making available to people what they want can hardly be an enemy of society. He is a benefactor of society. Not only so: He is at the mercy of other people as well. For if they refuse to buy what he produces he loses wealth and ends up penniless. On the other hand, why should people who purchase what someone else produces be envious of that producer's wealth because a million people buy his product? There is nothing to prevent them from competing with such a producer to share his market or to produce a similar commodity at a cheaper price, which will benefit the consumer even more.

What some purists object to is the production and sale of products they think to be deleterious to the buyers. After all, we do know that cigarette smoking and alcohol consumption are harmful. This is a fact. In a free society is it possible or is it useful for one group or another to determine what products should be made available to the consumer? After all, no one who thinks this way need produce or merchandize any product he thinks to be hazardous to health or well-being. The true locus of this problem arises when those who use products which are harmful look to society to pay for their care when disablement overtakes them. Why should I pay taxes to assist those who choose to destroy themselves when we know that the diseases connected with the consumption of alcohol and tobacco are self-inflicted, and that those who neither smoke nor drink do not fall prey to these diseases? That is the most difficult question of all. On the other hand, this is also a socialist problem because no socialist society has banished smoking and drinking. In fact the Soviet Union encourages the consumption of alcohol for the profit derived from the sale of such beverages.

What may be said of commodities pertaining to the individual may also be said of armaments which pertain to nations. On the face of it war makes no sense, and there would be none if all men were good. There have always been wars, and nothing on the horizon gives us reason to believe there will not be more of them. At any given time, around the world, there are wars, small and large. No one, however, can show that the right to private property is the root cause for war. Free enterprise countries *and* socialist countries are heavily armed. The socialist nations proclaim that imperialism is the worst of all evils and they expect to exterminate it by force. But what is stranger still is that socialist countries such as the Soviet Union and the People's Republic of China stand opposed to each other. And if socialist nations cannot be at peace with each other when the bourgeoisie of those nations have been eliminated and only the proletariat is left, the myth that socialism will bring in world peace is seen for what it really is.

Moreover, the advent of socialism and the destruction of the bourgeoisie do not guarantee that any nation so constituted will remain socialist. All of the socialist nations bemoan the rise of bourgeois sentiments and spend time and energy rooting them out. Human desire for private property cannot be eliminated from the hearts and minds of people, no matter how long socialism remains in power. Nor can the absence of human freedom be maintained, for this desire rises again and again amid the ashes of the totalitarian state which any socialist society must, of necessity, constitute.

In any event, this much we do know. Free enterprise more perfectly fulfills the cultural mandate to create wealth than does socialism. It is more consonant with human nature, so that of all the systems of economic life it will perform better in providing more goods for people everywhere. It can best insure that their wants be met and their material conditions improved. As long as men are men we can be sure they will want to improve their lot in life and will work toward that end. And they will always seek to create wealth for themselves. This is the reason why unrestrained and uncontrolled free enterprise will produce evils which lead to its condemnation and its replacement by socialism—which turns out to be a greater evil than free enterprise. And this is why the Judeo-Christian tradition, while it endorses free enterprise centering in private ownership of property, places controls on it along the lines we have described. The biblical stewardship mandate gives free enterprise a human face and governs the innate selfishness of men by requiring of them an altruism which fits the second table of the law, that we are to love our neighbors as we love ourselves.

[1]This is the Howard Zinn whose name was affixed to the large advertisement which appeared in *The Washington Post* on March 10, 1981 (A12). It was addressed to the U.S. Supreme Court and opened with this statement: "We, the undersigned, condemn the continued and escalating persecution of Bob Avakian, Chairman of the Central Committee of the Revolutionary Communist Party, and the 16 other Mao Tsetung Defendants." The statement was so bad that *The Washington Post* required some changes in the text. Professor Zinn is probably correct when he said he did not favor Russian socialism. This advertisement indicates an attachment to Maoism which may be even worse than an attachment to Russian socialism. The advertisement also carried the names of the Berrigan brothers, Harvey Cox of the Harvard Divinity School, and Robert McAfee Brown of the Pacific School of Religion in Berkeley, California.

ECONOMICS

HAVING TAKEN A LOOK AT THE QUESTION OF private property, we must now go on to the matter of economics. In this context, certain facts must be kept in mind constantly. The first has to do with capitalism or free enterprise.

When we speak here of free enterprise it may be roughly equated with what socialists call capitalism. While this is true, it needs to be reiterated that all socialist nations operate economically as capitalists. Since capitalism is common to free enterprise *and* to socialism, it is well for us to use the term free enterprise rather than capitalism. Socialist countries operate under what can only be termed state capitalism. The chief difference is that in free enterprise private ownership of the means of production is the rule of the game, while in socialism, state ownership of the means of production is the decisive factor. The negative consequences of state socialism will be elaborated later. Right now we will be talking about economics, first as it relates to features which are common to free enterprise and state capitalism or socialism, and then as it relates more specifically to free enterprise.

SELLING AND BUYING

Regardless of which economic system one embraces, people and nations must buy and sell commodities and services. This can be accomplished several ways. Goods and services can be bartered. For example, a seller of wheat can barter his wheat for clothes. The one who builds furniture can barter what he has made for food or clothing or whatever it is he wants. Buying and selling by barter is a tedious and time-consuming method. This is especially true if the seller of clothing first buys wheat which he doesn't want and then exchanges it for shoes which he really wants—but he cannot find anyone with shoes for sale who wants clothing.

For untold hundreds of years, money has been the medium which has supplanted the barter process. Traditionally gold and silver have been the chief media of exchange. All people have looked upon these metals as possessing a value which would enable them to sell one product to a buyer, and then use the gold or silver to buy something else in turn, which the buyer of the first product did not have to sell. Gold gradually became legal tender in and among nations.

In America, President Franklin Delano Roosevelt demonetized gold. Until this happened the United States printed paper money which could be redeemed by gold. The gold was held in vaults and was a guarantee that the paper money was backed by something all people were willing to accept as a medium of exchange. So long as this condition existed, paper money was useful. But when gold was demonetized (and more recently silver, for the coins now in use contain no silver and are not redeemable for either silver or gold), the situation was not appreciably changed—so long as Americans and foreigners who sold goods for paper money had "faith" in that paper money. But when government began printing more paper money than holders of that money had confidence in, paper money began to lose its value. It then required more paper money to purchase the same amount of goods. This process can continue until the paper money is virtually valueless and people go back to barter, or to a new "hard" paper money system, or revert to the gold and silver standard.

Whatever the method of exchange may be, there are other factors in the exchange of goods and services which are common to free enterprise and socialism. One important factor has to do with value. Commodities have no value unless they have two characteristics. First, they must be marketable, i.e., somebody must want them. Second, they must have cost some labor to produce. Any commodity which has these two characteristics has value. The absence of one of them means the commodity does not have value. The man who spends a lifetime writing a book nobody buys or reads has nothing of value. Likewise the person who has a commodity which lacks utility has nothing of value. Air does not involve labor, nor do the light and heat of the sun. Therefore they have no value so far as selling them as a commodity is concerned.

When something has value it means someone has something to sell that someone else is willing to buy. When the value of what is for sale is to be determined, the law of supply and demand prevails. This law operates in free enterprise and socialism. Simply, it means that both seller and buyer must be satisfied before the exchange takes place. The buyer will not make his purchase until he can get the commodity for what he thinks it is worth to him. And the seller will not sell until he gets the price for the commodity which he thinks it is worth. The actual selling price is not particularly significant because both parties are satisfied.

In socialist countries, this market principle can be altered by the use of wage and price controls and other devices such as central planning, which includes the making of decisions not on the basis of what people want, but according to what the state thinks they need and ought to have. But when the socialist countries engage in international trade they cannot avoid the principle involved in any true transaction. The Soviet Union, for example, cannot sell to people in the United States what nobody will buy. And the United States cannot buy what the Soviet Union does not wish to sell. Only when the buyer is satisfied with the price, and the seller is satisfied with what he will receive for what he sells, does the transaction take place.

In the exchange of goods and services the inevitable question of profits arises. Obviously no one can sell commodities for less than what it costs to produce them and remain solvent for any length of time. This is true for free enterprise and socialism. Socialism condemns profits and criticizes the profit motive. Socialism is forever trying to make people believe that the profit motive is somehow evil and should be abolished. But no socialist society can survive for long without the profit motive. There are several reasons for this.

Any socialist country which sold its goods and services for no more than the cost of producing them would stand still. There would be no improvement in the economic well-being of its people. There would be no additional housing, no increase in business, no accumulation of capital without which there can be no economic progress (as we shall see again later). New factories could not be built, new products could not be introduced, and the material life style of the people could not be enhanced.

Socialist countries are just as profit-minded as any nation in which free enterprise flourishes. The difference is this: In socialist countries the state, rather than the individual, reaps the profits and determines how they will be used. In the process, freedom is sacrificed and human rights annulled. The socialist people are enslaved. What is worse yet is that the socialists abdicate their own economic theories and in doing so prove themselves to be unconscionably hypocritical.

Adam Smith said that "The value which the workers add to their materials resolves itself into two parts of which one pays their wages and the other is the profit of the employer." It is precisely because of the accuracy of this statement that socialism proclaims the capitalist to be guilty of thievery. Marx argued that the workers produced the profit which the employers stole from them. He called it surplus value rather than profits and said it was obtained by exploiting the workers. But what do we find among the socialist countries?

Since there can be no betterment of the economic situation of anyone without surplus value or profits, it becomes plain that in socialist countries the worker is still deprived of the fruits of his labor if the Marxist view is correct. This time, however, it is the state which takes the surplus value and uses it as the leadership of the state decides, rather than what the people and the multitude of capitalists would choose to do in free enterprise. Socialist workers do not get what they are supposed to in socialist theory unless one takes seriously the myth that the people are the state and the state is the people. When it is seen that the Communist party in the Soviet Union comprises only a small segment of the total population, this myth takes on the semblance of the ridiculous.

Still another factor which is common to both systems we are discussing is the dictum that the consumer is king. No matter who produces what, the response of the consumer to what is offered for sale will determine what happens. The American automobile industry recently learned this lesson to its sorrow. In 1980 the Big Three, GM, Ford, and Chrysler, posted the largest losses in their history. Foreign imports based on small car psychology favored by the consumers gained sales, while the American producers of gas guzzlers lost them. The market lesson is as old as economic history. Unless the sellers produce what the buyers want, they will not sell them anything. This is likewise true in socialist countries with a minor reservation. When socialist countries produce inferior goods and fail to supply the consumers with what they want, they do not sell their products. The reservation, of course, lies in the fact that socialist countries do not allow for competition with the state. There are no alternatives to Soviet shoes of inferior quality, but the fact that the shoes are inferior often leaves warehouses filled with unsold inventories. When free enterprise failures occur, the state does not pay the losses, whereas when socialist failures occur all of the people pay the price.

Some Americans have written passionately about what they feel to be the great injustice perpetrated on the banana-producing countries of Central America. They have spoken harshly about the multinational corporations which have control of the banana market, saying that the workers have been exploited, and the profits from the industry have been reaped by America rather than by the Central American peoples themselves.

First, it may be said that the economic conditions among the peoples of the chief banana-producing countries are bad. Second, it remains to be proved that the profits reaped by the multinational companies is exorbitant. Third, it has not been shown that the profits which have been taken out of the country are disproportionate to the investment involved, and to the monies which remain in the country for further development. What then is the real issue and what lies at the heart of the problem?

Any nation whose economy is built on a single product or two or three products is open to intense and frequent economic difficulties, unless the product or products they offer are in great demand. In buying and selling we must remember that the consumer is king. Bananas are worth what buyers will pay for them—no more and no less. Bananas never will be a product which commands a price tag that will make any nation rich. They are not a product people must have. As soon as the price reaches a certain point there are fewer buyers. And that point is a low one. After all, anyone can try to sell bananas for a hundred dollars each. But he will not find many buyers. There is nothing in bananas of such intrinsic worth which would make them an item people will spend that kind of money to obtain.

If we compare bananas with coffee and oil, the difference is striking. People want coffee and oil. So necessary are these to the desires of the consumer that he will pay much larger sums proportionately to secure them. Most people can do without bananas and always will when the price is not right. Thus it is imprudent and economically suicidal to build a national economy on bananas. This has nothing whatever to do with ethics, compassion, or a passionate concern for the livelihood of a people. Markets do not take those factors into account and never will. And in times of economic stress when people's purchasing power is limited, we can be sure that bananas will be low on the list of what they will buy when compared with other things they really want. No one has ever been deprived by having to do without bananas.

The market solution for the banana countries is to change their economic base and begin producing other commodities for which there is a far greater demand. They must also diversify their production so that, humanly speaking, they will always have something needed by consumers that they will place high on their priority list.

And what can be said about Central American nations can also be said about Cuba. This country has based a large part of its economy on sugar. Sugar is a desired and marketable commodity. But when a nation's economy is concentrated on a commodity as valuable as sugar it is often possible to run into difficulties which have serious repercussions. In the case of Cuba, sugar plant disease has hurt its economy. However, the country does have tobacco and is famous for its cigars. But typical socialist inefficiency has hampered the nation, and its economic future appears bleak unless and until free enterprise is again introduced into that country.

EQUALITARIANISM AND THE MARKETPLACE

One of the chief characteristics of socialism is its notion of human equalitarianism. This is implicit in the socialist slogan: Everyone was to be paid according to his need and each worker was to contribute according to his ability. This idea was not invented by Marx and his contemporaries. It has a long history in the affairs of mankind. The Pilgrim Fathers tried this experiment when they settled in New England. The practice of this principle brought them close to disaster and threatened the very life of the community. Once the fathers reverted to free enterprise the colony prospered and the threat of starvation was eliminated.

When Russia was sovietized by the communists, Nicolai Lenin tried the equalitarian approach. The use of the approach divorced a man's pay from his productivity. Human nature being what it is, Lenin quickly discovered the error inherent in the theory. He commenced the Five Year Plans in which variations in the value of the work were recognized and pay scale differentials were established. In Stalin's day, factory managers in World War II were getting wages ten times that of the workers. Will Rogers, who had a keen sense of humor, said that he liked Russia very much because he could find no communists there. That is, they paid lip service to principles they did not practice and which would never allow them to succeed if they did. The socialist equalitarian principle has never worked before and will not work now.

Before the Russian revolution, as we mentioned previously, the farmers of that country produced enough food to supply the entire nation and to export food as well. When the Soviets expropriated the farms and starved millions of the Kulaks it sounded the death knell to agriculture. From a surplus-producing nation, the Soviet Union became a grain-importing nation—and the situation has not improved in recent years. The inbuilt inefficiency of socialism caught up quickly with the Soviets.

Pragmatism overtook the Soviets as a result of their farm problems. They allocate small patches of land to farmers who are free to work these plots in addition to their servitude on the state farms. These small plots produce more agricultural products than do the state farms, because they are intensively cultivated and the farmers enjoy what is a modicum of free enterprise, since they are permitted to sell their vegetables to Russians who wish to buy them. This practice has its values, first, because it exposes the fallacy of socialism for all who have eyes to see. Second, it encourages shreds of free enterprise which may bear a rich harvest for the time when the system may be overthrown. The third advantage lies in the dependence of the Soviet Union on the Western democracies, notably the United States and Canada, to supply it with food. The importance of this dependency should not be overlooked at a time when the world is faced with the possibility of a nuclear holocaust. The Soviets do not really want to kill off the capitalist nations by warfare. They prefer surrender. If, for example, the United States was defeated by extensive use of nuclear bombs, the land would be useless for agricultural purposes for a long time. Meanwhile the Soviets would have victory at the price of starvation for themselves. Detente and Salt agreements which enable them to achieve military superiority are understandable. When the time comes and the balance of power has shifted sufficiently in favor of the Soviet Union, their leaders probably hope that the threat of force will be enough to bring the United States to its knees.

Some people do not think that food should be a weapon even in a war for survival. The foolishness of this is apparent if for no other reason than that there are multitudes of people everywhere who would like to improve their situation by securing the food withheld from the Soviet Union by the Western world.

PROFITS

Marx argued that labor alone creates value. Therefore the profits which the employer makes are derived from the work for which the laborers are not paid. He said this is unjust unless the workers get the full return for their labors. Marx was mistaken in this opinion, as anyone with any economic sense must realize. The employer must invest capital in his plant where the worker labors. When the product has been made and is ready for sale there are selling costs which must be included in the value, that is, the price for which the goods are sold. Usually there is a middleman who acts as distributor for the manufacturer. Then there is the merchant who sells the goods to the consumer. The manufacturer is entitled to a return on his investment in land and buildings and machinery.

Labor alone does not create the value of the product. But that leaves open the question of how much profit the manufacturer is entitled to receive for his product. This is a hard question for which there are no easy answers. For example, the manufacturer may not be able to sell all the goods he has produced. The cost of the unsold goods must be taken into account when the sales price is set. Moreover, the manufacturer is the risk taker. The worker receives his wages whether the product is sold or not. The manufacturer is gambling and has to take into account a number of factors.

First, the manufacturer must gamble that he has a product people want. Second, he must gamble that he will be able to sell it at a price the consumers are willing to pay. Third, he is always faced with competition from other manufacturers who may produce goods of equal or better quality at a cheaper price. Moreover, he is caught up in a world of rapid change in which his product may be superseded by progress and made useless by new inventions. There was no market for buggy whips from the moment the automobile became the number one means of transportation. Rail transportation has lost much of its passenger traffic to the airplane. So it goes.

When buyers and sellers work with a market economy, the selling price of a commodity may vary widely and thus the profit will too. Some artists paint canvasses which sell for a fortune. Others can get a mere hundred or two hundred dollars for paintings which took as much time and skill as those which bring the highest prices. The price is related to the demand, and the profit differential between cost of production and selling price may vary greatly.

Prices also vary greatly depending on the number of the particular objects which are being sold. A handmade suit varies in price from those made in a factory in large numbers. A handcrafted automobile must cost more to produce than one produced on an assembly line operation. The sales prices will reflect these differences. It is a rule of thumb that the more the manufacturer produces of a product the less the unit cost of production, and the cheaper the selling price. The market economy has a way of balancing out value or prices, but at all times there may be opportunities for sellers to achieve what some would call excess profits. What do we say to this?

First we must ask whether there is such a thing as excess profits. Are there ethical and moral values which belong intrinsically to the market place? Laissez faire capitalism, and socialism for that matter too, would not bring to bear on free enterprise the morality of the Old and New Testaments. Both of these systems are rooted in the Enlightenment in which the second table of the

Law is not accepted—that is, "Thou shalt love thy neighbor as thyself." Therefore the question of profit is one-sidedly based upon whatever the buyer is willing to pay and nothing more. How does this work?

One can illustrate the problem this way. One man has more food than he needs for survival for himself and his family. Others in the community for a variety of reasons have nothing to eat in a time of famine. Various people wish to buy food from him. Some offer large sums of money for his food. Others offer little or nothing, depending on their economic status. He knows that some will starve if they get no food. If he sells the food to the highest bidders he will help himself the most. In any event, the ones to whom he does not sell food will die. Even if he chooses to sell his surplus food on the basis of considerations other than money, the net result will be identical. Some will die and some will live. It is difficult to make the choice in such a case on a moral or strictly ethical basis. The pragmatic aspect would appear to be equally legitimate. There cannot be anything necessarily wrong with selling the food to those who are willing to pay the highest price.

In the case just mentioned we may well ask whether the highest price might still be the wrong basis on which to make the choice to sell. If it were diamonds or clothing or something else that would not make the difference between life and death, the case of the highest bidder would appear to be unquestionable. But when we are talking about what is essential to life itself, it is difficult to suppose that one should take advantage of a situation to set a price which goes far beyond reason. Here the law of love of neighbor is part of the situation, but how can one impose the Judeo-Christian viewpoint on those who do not accept it to begin with? In general then, the law of supply and demand constitutes the working basis for selling and buying. There are some instances, however, when this law should be superseded by the law of love.

Profit is of the essence in free enterprise, as has been stated. It is also essential to socialism, though covered over cleverly by semantics. It is always the result of producing more than you consume. The need for, and importance of, profit cannot be overestimated. The world population is expected to increase by more than two billion people before the end of this century. The human needs of more than six billion people will have to be met. If we think of the production of goods and services as a giant pie we can understand the necessity for greater production of goods and services. If the size of the pie is reduced or remains the same there are only two possibilities open to men. Any disbalance can be altered by redistribution for the benefit of the have-nots and reducing the supply of goods and services available to the more affluent. When the population increases, and the size of the pie does not increase or grows smaller, then it is clear that there will be less for just about everybody except, perhaps, for a very small minority.

If there is not enough food to care for the human needs of the world right now, then it follows that with the increase of population expected by the end of the century, the food situation will worsen considerably. People will starve in greater numbers than ever before. The only way in which this can be remedied is for people to increase the production of food. The increase must be greater than the consumption. In other words, there must be more produced than is now consumed if more mouths are to be fed. When more is produced than the producers consume, profit exists.

If the additional food cannot be produced profitably, the producers will go bankrupt. If there is no profit, and only the threat of a loss, there is no incentive to increase production. The same conditions inhere for clothing, transportation, communication, education, police protection, and the other items which are required for the sustaining of life. Profit or wealth is required to meet the necessities of life. The size of the pie must be increased. Any increase means an increase in wealth. And any increase in wealth means profit.

PROFITS AND THE SOVIET BLOC

One of the most interesting developments in the economic realm has been the socialist method of doing business with the capitalist or free enterprise nations. Everything which the socialist nations purchase from the capitalist countries must be paid for. This is no secret. Everyone knows that the American farmer must be paid for his wheat and corn. And manufacturers must be paid for their products so that they, in turn, can pay their employees and their stockholders. All of this is obvious. But what is not so obvious is the way in which this trade is promoted.

We can begin by observing the behavior of the Soviet Union itself. The ruble is not the medium of exchange used in international trade by the Soviets. It is not tradable and cannot be exchanged for dollars except at a rate which penalizes whoever holds rubles. Sellers of commodities do not want rubles. They want U.S. dollars or gold and silver. But the Soviets do not want to use gold and silver to make their purchases. If they did, they would soon be without gold or silver. So how do they make their purchases? They do so by obtaining credit from the very nations who sell them their goods.

Recently it was calculated that the Soviet Union owes forty or more billions of dollars to the West in credits extended to the nation for the purchase of Western goods. Any number of Western observers have stated that technically the Soviet Union is bankrupt. The billions it has borrowed from the West to pay for Western goods comes from the wealth of these nations. Credit is more than a bookkeeping arrangement. The actual medium of exchange must be available to pay for the goods purchased. So the profits earned by the West are borrowed to pay for the goods. Why does the West do this?

The West extends credit to the Soviet Union because if it did not, its goods might not be sold and the West would suffer economic attrition. The temporary advantage is obvious so far as the West is concerned. And so long as the farmers are paid for their crops they really care little about who has loaned the Soviets the money to pay for the goods. Nor do the large corporations who sell technical machinery and sophisticated electronic equipment to the Soviets. All they care about is that they are paid for their goods and can in turn pay their employees and stockholders, and generate some profit.

It is estimated that the banks and other agencies which hold out the golden bag to the Soviets are the ones who face ruination in the event the Soviets do not pay their debts. And it is more than likely that they will not. Again and again their indebtedness is refinanced so that they are only paying interest on the indebtedness, not on the principal. The Soviet intention is to take over the democracies, more particularly the United States, and when they do that there will be no need to pay any of those debts. In other words, the Western nations are giving the Soviets the rope by which they themselves will be hung when the time comes.

If it were not for the credit extended to the Soviets by the West, the Soviet Union would be in no shape to wage war, build armies and navies, and stockpile missiles. If the Soviets had to pay cash on the barrelhead for the food alone which they import, it would have a dramatic effect on their budget and their expenditures on military apparatus.

Cuba is one nation which best illustrates the inefficiency of socialism and the stupidity of the West. Cuba is an economic basket case. Despite the glowing reports which have been written by socialist advocates, Cuba is in desperate straits. It is amusing that Castro constantly blames the United States for his nation's plight. He has in mind the embargo which prevents goods from the United States being shipped to Cuba. The Soviet Union is the nation which keeps Cuba afloat economically. And this nation does so because Cuba plays a strategic role in Soviet expansionism. Cuban troops are fighting all over Africa today. And the Cuban nation itself is the recipient of a subsidy of at least a billion dollars a year from the Soviets.

Americans and everyone else should realize that the American embargo has nothing whatever to do with the horrendous economic situation of Cuba. There is virtually nothing the United States could sell to Cuba which cannot be purchased from other nations which sell similar goods and services. Why don't the Cubans buy these goods and services from the other nations? The answer is easily perceived. Cuba does not have the funds with which to do so; it is a bankrupt nation. And the socialist system has faltered so gravely that there is no hope in the future for the Cubans to develop the resources with which to pay for the goods and services it needs from the West. Only if credit were extended to Cuba would the nation be able to make the necessary purchases. But Cuba is hardly a safe risk, and few indeed are the capitalists stupid enough to extend credit they know will never be paid back.

The lesson is apparent enough for all to see. Cuba is in worse financial shape than it ever was under its former rulers and their dictatorial type of economic control. What Cuba needs more than anything else is a blood transfusion of free enterprise which would put it back on its economic feet. There is little likelihood of this except by the opposite kind of revolution to the one pulled off by Castro some years ago.

The Polish issue is equally significant. But it must be remembered that Poland is still not a typical illustration of a true socialist state. The government has not yet been able to expropriate the land from the farmers. They still own their farmlands. And there are minor forms of capitalism coexisting with state socialism. The Soviet Union artfully milks its satellite nations such as Poland of their resources to meet its own needs. It takes more from these conquered nations than it returns to them. The nations consume less than they produce and the Soviets keep the difference. It might be put this way: The Soviets take what they want, and the people live on what the Soviets leave behind them.

Poland today has an indebtedness to the West which runs far more than twenty billion dollars. The nation has little or nothing with which to pay for goods purchased from the West. Yet it needs what the West has to offer. Credit is the only way in which Poland can make these purchases. And once again we see an instance in which the wealth that is the profits of the West, must be extended to Poland to keep it afloat economically. The Soviet Union isn't going to do it.

Even while this is being written Poland is undergoing a critical economic crisis in which the workers are rebelling against their socialist masters. It is relatively easy to predict the outcome of this struggle. The Soviet Union will prevail. It has no intention whatever of releasing Poland from its bondage. Every effort will be made to quell the dissidents without the use of armed force. But if it can be brought about by no other means than the use of force, then force will be employed. The Soviets will surely try first to use indigenous Polish armed might if at all possible. But if this does not work, then the Soviet military machine will strike ruthlessly and effectively. And the West will stand by and do nothing.

PROFITS AND THE U.S. NATIONAL DEBT

Having dealt with the Soviet bloc and its use of capitalist wealth to pay for its purchases of goods and services from the West, we now must look at what is happening in the United States as well. The place to start is to look at the problem of inflation and the decline of the American dollar in the world market.

America can buy all it wants from other nations so long as it has a medium of exchange to use for its purchases which is acceptable to the sellers. For decades the dollar has been the world's basic money medium for virtually all nations. Today the value of the dollar has eroded so severely that it may be on its way out as a medium of exchange. Every time the dollar declines on the international currency market, *vis a vis* the currencies of Switzerland, West Germany, and Japan, the holders of American dollars soon discover that it takes more of them to purchase goods from these countries. Those who hold dollars continue to lose purchasing power so long as this condition persists. Loss of purchasing power means a loss of wealth, or a diminishing of profit. This is an important factor in international trade.

The same problem exists on the home front in America. The nation now has a national debit of more than 1.1 trillion dollars and in a short time it will exceed that amount. This will be, possibly, the largest national debt any nation has ever incurred. What does it mean?

In the United States the government alone can print paper money which has no intrinsic value in itself. Why does it not print more paper money and pay off the national debt? The answer is obvious enough. Bad money drives out good money. Paper money, which is not backed up by something intrinsically valuable to all to whom the United States owes money, quickly sinks in value. Germany, after World War I, learned this lesson the hard way. It reached a point where one needed a wheelbarrow to carry to the store the millions of German marks which it cost to buy a loaf of bread. Ernest Henderson, the founder of the famed Sheraton chain of hotels, wrote about Germany's great inflation after World War I. He said: "With German marks on the toboggan, the invoice price of eight hundred million marks on which duty would be assessed [for German goods he was importing] and shrunk so drastically in terms of our money that the twenty-percent levy was now only two dollars and forty cents, by the time there were funds for meeting this formality" *(The World of "Mr. Sheraton,"* Ernest Henderson, N.Y., 1962, p. 44). At the rate stated above, a twenty-cent loaf of bread would have cost sixty-seven million marks! Eventually this ruinous financial plight helped to bring about the rise of Adolf Hitler and his totalitarian regime, which brought on World War II.

Where, then, did the United States get the money which made possible the national debt of more than 900 billion dollars in 1980? The response is not difficult to understand. It borrowed the money from investors who had surplus funds, profit if you please, which they were willing to lend the government. The government became one of the prime rivals for the use of private capital to pay its bills. It was doing what business and wage earners cannot do very long. It was consuming more than it produced by taxes. The only way it could pay its bills was to borrow money. And the private sector was the only place to borrow the money. The money itself was savings or profits, for they are one and the same.

When two things happen together—the increase of the national debt and inflation—a curious consequence results. As the value of the dollar drops, the true amount of the national debt tends to decline. If a national debt of a billion dollars will buy a third of a million bushels of wheat, that's one thing. But when a larger debt of five billion dollars ten years later will buy only the same number of bushels of wheat, it is easy to see that the government will be paying back its debt in dollars which have a lower purchasing power than the dollars it originally borrowed. The saver loses purchasing power; i.e., the government by deliberately encouraging inflation reduces its own indebtedness by stealing the purchasing power of the people from whom it borrowed the money.

The growth of the American national debt is relatively insignificant when compared to what the government has done with respect to social security. Private pension arrangements are closely monitored and are subject to considerable federal regulation. So are all kinds of insurance companies required to conform to government regulations. Wherever the private sector operates, the government requires that adequate reserves be set aside for all contingencies. But when it comes to Social Security, this principle has been abandoned by the federal government. The system is so seriously underfunded that it would require trillions of dollars to bring it up to the requirements set for privately owned companies in the same business.

At this moment, workers are paying into the Social Security system monies which are being distributed immediately to retired workers. Even then, the amount of money coming into the system by employee and employer contributions is less than the amount being paid out. Thus the reserves soon will be exhausted. The United Press International under a November 10, 1980, dateline released a report that came from the congressional Joint Economic Committee. This committee reported that the fund's reserve levels "will be inadequate to maintain the cash flow of the program by later 1981 or early 1982." In plain English it means that the final reserves will have been eaten up and there will be no reserves left to pay the retired workers on Social Security, except for the less than sufficient yearly income received by the government from working people. The workers' money will be used to pay some, not all, of the benefits for other people, and nothing will be maintained in reserve to pay the pensions of present workers when they retire.

The government by devious devices has squandered the reserves formerly held in trust by the Social Security System. Some have been used for other than the purposes for which they were collected. Additional benefits were legislated for retirees and other programs such as Medicare were instituted without making provision for their funding. A decade ago a magazine like *Christianity Today* was criticized when it editorialized about the coming Social Security crisis. Defenders claimed there were adequate reserves for as long as needed. Unrealistic figures of prospective income were adduced to show the system would receive far more funds in the future than were needed to guarantee the actuarial soundness of the plan. This was legerdemain that had no basis in fact.

In substance the Social Security debacle amounts to a theft of the wealth of the subscribers to the system, that is, the theft of their savings or, if you please, their profits or surplus funds. Most workers have no choice about Social Security. It is mandated for them by Congress. It is a welfare scheme and should be so titled, as such it is part of the growing welfare state which has for its central principle the redistribution of wealth. This is part of the very nature of socialism in which the few decide for the many and freedom is lost.

PROFIT AND HOME MORTGAGES

Profits make possible the accumulation of wealth. This is called capital formation. It is essential to economic growth and to the improvement of the economic condition of all. This can be demonstrated in numberless ways.

One illustration is housing. The Soviet Union, with all of its vaunted praise of socialism and its denigration of capitalism or free enterprise, has failed notably in producing adequate housing for its people. The apartments provided for workers cannot be compared with those in the West. First, they turn out to be slums without adequate plumbing and a lack of space which confines families to two or three rooms. Nor are there enough apartments to go around, so that people wait years before they can find what at best is inadequate and substandard housing. Under capitalism Americans are among the best housed people in the world. Why is this and what makes it possible?

Under free enterprise housing mortgages are made possible by capital accumulation by people who lend their money to savings and loan associations, among others. These savings are then made available to homeowners who do not have sufficient funds to buy houses outright. They borrow what they need from different lending companies. They pay interest on what they borrow and repay the principal in twenty or thirty years. If housing loan money is not available, people cannot buy houses. The only way for mortgage money to become available is for people to accumulate capital (that is, to create wealth) and allow it to be used for such purposes as this.

In order to attract money for deposit, savings and loan associations must pay the saver an attractive rate of interest in order for him to deposit his money in the associations. The lender must charge the borrower a higher rate of interest than it pays the depositor so that it can continue in business and make a profit. This middleman function is important. It performs a service whereby hundreds of small depositors can lend the association enough money to make large loans possible. Few depositors are able to save enough capital to make loans on their own, that is, to go into the lending business themselves.

There is no socialist nation in existence where workers can do what the workers in free America can do. Independence through home ownership and the accumulation of capital is made possible by a system which enables workers to consume less than they earn and leave a balance for them to improve their economic situation. In no socialist state is this possible. But there is more to capital formation than home mortgages.

CAPITAL FORMATION AND BUSINESS

The only way a business can develop and enlarge its operations is by capital formation. To this end the device which has contributed to modern free enterprise or capitalism is the corporation. If someone has an idea he wishes to develop, it takes capital to do so. There are several ways in which this capital can be secured. One way is to sell stock in a corporation set up by the entrepreneur. This means that whoever has capital can invest in the company in a large or a small way. Millions of Americans have become capitalists by buying stock in companies which the stockholders then own and control. They have good reason to protect their investment by rejecting socialism and promoting free enterprise. For if socialism came into being the producing companies would be expropriated by the state and the investors would lose their stake in the company or companies.

Another way to begin a company would be to borrow money from a bank or some other source without resorting to the sale of stock. The company would pay interest on the money borrowed and perhaps even include a provision by which the lender received a share of the profits, if there were any.

Still another way in which much of America's modern industry was built was by the enterprise of individuals who set up small shops or plants using their own capital.

Profits from the small unit would be reinvested in the company to enlarge its productive capacity. After a period of time it might develop into a large organization without having had to sell stock or borrow money from banks and investors. A needleworker might spend time at night making clothes for sale. And his wife might do the same. They would scrimp and save so that they could buy a sewing machine, so as to produce more than they could produce by hand. Together they saved more money so that they could buy another sewing machine to produce more clothing to sell. Then they saved enough to buy a third sewing machine and hired someone to work for them. In twenty years they became a large clothing manufacturing company with two hundred workers, a factory building, and a sales force. The founders had become millionaires. This is anybody's story in a nation where free enterprise exists. But it is an impossible accomplishment in a socialist nation.

One can illustrate this sort of system from the Old and New Testaments without finding one word of criticism about the system of free enterprise. In the Gospel of St. Mark the calling of James and John to join Jesus is recorded. They were engaged in the fishing business with their father. It was more than a family affair. The statement is made:

And straightway he called them: and they left their father Zebedee in the ship with the hired servants and went with him.

Here is the illustration of a fisherman who succeeded in business and found it necessary and profitable to hire men to assist him in his craft. It was free enterprise at work.

In the famed story of the Prodigal Son we are told that when this man came to his senses, having spent his inheritance in frivolous living, he said:

*I will arise and go to my father, and will say unto him,
Father, I have sinned against heaven and before thee,
and am no more worthy to be called your son: make me
as one of thy hired servants.*

There is still another instance of a successful farmer
whose enterprise enabled him to hire workers to assist
him. No word of rebuke is spoken by Jesus about the
bourgeois owner and his sinfulness for exploiting his proletariat workers. Nor is there a word of reproof against
the rich man in the Gospel of Mark, who employed a
steward to look after his wealth. Nor does Jesus condemn this rich man for lending his substance to others
for a fee and expecting to be repaid. In each and every
case these people of whom Jesus speaks were engaged in
free enterprise and in the creation of wealth, an endeavor which enabled them to hire people who otherwise
might not have had any work by which to live.

Needless to say, the profit and loss motive has for its
only effective alternative a totalitarian state. At the
same time we must remember that free enterprise is a
profit *and loss* system. For everyone who succeeds there
are others who fail and who remain workers rather than
owners. Yet workers can become capitalists through
their savings, which they can invest in a variety of ways.

THE ROLE OF GOVERNMENT

Free enterprise supposes the existence of a market economy which operates according to economic laws. But
any market economy can be altered, abridged, or rendered partially ineffective by what the government of a
nation does. When the government intervenes in the
marketplace it always has a negative effect on the normal
operations of a free enterprise system. The ways in
which a government can intervene in a marketplace are
many and devious. What are some of them?

Parkinson's law always operates in government. Briefly stated it is this: Over a period of time the number of employees will double while the work load remains the same. In other words, it will take twice as many people to do the same work that half as many did a decade or two decades before. Moreover, the size of government never decreases except momentarily. Over the long haul it always goes up. A bureaucracy always comes into existence which has for its major purpose maintaining itself and increasing in size. To do so it must offer a rationale, the most famous of which is the need to provide more and more services for the people. Thus the bureaucracy has to devise more and more plans and methods by which to spend money and to increase the amount to be spent. Thomas Jefferson recognized the danger of this when he said:

I place economy among the first and most important virtues, and public debt as the greatest of dangers . . . we must take our choice between economy and liberty, or profusion and servitude. If we can prevent the government from wasting the labors of the people under the pretense of caring for them, they will be happy.

The larger the government bureaucracy grows the more it must intervene in the operations of the marketplace and the more damage it does. Under the pretense of caring for the people it has established in America the Social Security System, of which we have already spoken. (Not that there is any objection to such a scheme if it were properly funded.) It has set up innumerable agencies to police, regulate, and otherwise interfere with business. Mountains of paper forms must be filled out, suits by the government against private citizens engaged in business operations becloud the courts, and inspectors like flies in summertime are found lurking in the corridors of large and small business buildings and plants.

Government has so entrenched itself in the financial life of the nation that it has meddled in ways undreamed of by the founders of the nation who wrote the Constitution. Two major corporations have been bailed out by the government in recent years — Lockheed and Chrysler. In both cases the argument was advanced that government intervention with financial guarantees was needed in order to keep the industry competitive and to keep unemployment from rising. The government also bailed out New York City, which was guilty of violating virtually every sound economic law known to man. When government interferes in this manner it becomes, in effect, owner and operator of the enterprise which then is subject to external and internal control by the government which has rescued it.

The recent creation of an Education Department of the government with cabinet status indicates the penetration of the federal apparatus into the operations of the smallest one-room schoolhouse in some remote rural county seat. Added to this is the penetration of the government into the health service field through Medicare and Medicaid and the prospect that it will eventually control a national health care program which will cover people from the womb to the tomb. Joined onto this are such items as food stamps, loans to college students (with the subsequent intervention of the government into the operations of the institutions themselves), affirmative action programs, bussing, abortion, civil rights, and an almost innumerable number of other matters which impinge on the rights of the states and the citizenry of the nation. This is not to say that these items are of no interest and concern to the people. Rather, the evil rises from the increasingly extensive interference in the lives of all citizens at the hands of what now has become the master of the people rather than their servant.

Particularly in the economic arena, the intervention of

government has brought malevolent results. Its greatest crime is related to its ability to expand the amount of credit available to those who want to borrow money. So long as the size of the money supply roughly equals the real amount of wealth or savings, there is no problem. It is true, of course, that the business cycle is an inbuilt economic corrective which pulls businessmen up short when they disobey the economic laws known to men. Recessions, or depressions, as they were formerly called, function in a way which brings men back to economic basics. But when the government intervenes by making available more credit than the actual wealth of the nation mandates, the troubles mount. How does government extend the amount of credit available?

The overexpansion of the money supply can be brought about by a variety of means. The government can resort to the printing press to put out more paper money. If it were possible to create wealth by printing paper money, all the economic problems of life would be virtually resolved. But when more and more paper money which has no real wealth quality begins to circulate, it loses value. Whoever receives the money first has a distinct advantage because the relationship between the supply of money and the goods available is not distorted when the cycle begins. But as the paper money works its way through the economy, prices escalate and the paper money increasingly loses some or all of its purchasing power.

Rising prices do not mean that the value of the purchased goods has increased. Rather they indicate that the value of the paper money has decreased. In America today, homes which formerly cost twenty thousand dollars are selling in some places for two hundred thousand dollars. Milk which formerly cost fifteen cents a quart now sells for more than fifty cents a quart. Whoever buys milk or homes does not have more purchasing power because the prices are higher. In some instances the higher prices only reflect the fact that the real wealth has declined, not increased.

The government can also increase the number of dollars through the Federal Reserve System, which has the power to tighten or loosen the financial noose. The more the number of paper dollars released through the decisions of the Federal Reserve Banking System, the greater will be the inflationary spiral. As prices go up, if the money supply does not increase it will bring about an economic crisis which is nothing more than the operation of the free market economy to make an adjustment for the mistake of printing too much money.

Government itself faces a crisis when the expansion of the currency brings about economic slowdown. Unemployment increases, goods begin to pile up in the warehouses, and economic activity slows down. The consumer is caught up in the consequences which flow from this slowdown and economic woes begin to increase. Government is then faced with a choice of letting nature take its course until the inflationary effects have been squeezed out of the system, or by stimulating the faltering economy by adding still more dollars to the pot. In late 1979 when the United States was on the edge of a significant recession, Mr. Volcker, the chief of the Federal Reserve, made the statement: ". . . higher inflation means the Fed must supply more money to sustain economic activity." This frightening statement has implications which are plain enough. It is like adding gasoline to a fire.

The 1979-80 recession was caused by the expansion of the currency. Even Keynes, whose economic theories are now held in suspicion by most informed economists, said that a nation can be broken by the overuse of the printing press to put paper money into the marketplace. When a recession is caused by increasing the money supply beyond proper limits, it would seem to be self-evident that adding still further to the number of dollars in circulation is hardly the solution to the problem. Politicians, however, when faced with unpleasant choices, always yield to the very situation which caused the problem in the first place. So the government eases the credit crunch by increasing the money supply after a period of time, during which the free market had begun to adjust to the situation. When the money supply is increased before the free market has had full opportunity to correct the imbalance, prices begin to rise again. In turn this leads to another recession sooner or later, and each succeeding recession adds to the already existing woes. This process of solving recessions by adding to the money supply which produces another recession can only lead at last to the complete destruction of the currency of this or any nation.

History affords us with example after example of nations whose currencies have been completely destroyed by government intervention in the economic realm. When this happens the people who are least able to protect themselves suffer the most. Inflation itself victimizes the retired on fixed incomes, and depreciates the wealth of those whose holdings are in savings banks and bonds. Inflation is a hidden form of taxation which seriously affects multitudes of people who are ignorant of the implications and either do not know how to protect themselves or simply fail to do so. Moreover workers whose pension funds are invested in assets which do not keep pace with the inflationary spiral will retire with incomes having lower purchasing power than the dollars they invested in their pension account, as will the dollars contributed by the companies for whom they labored.

Economists speak of *lag time*, which is the period of time between the increase in the money supply and the moment when the increase has fully affected prices. In the United States in earlier recessions the lag time was two or three years. But in countries like Chile, Argentina, and Brazil the lag time right now is only a few weeks. Each succeeding recession in America reduces the lag time and increases what is called the velocity of money. There is other bad news for the unhappy victims of inflation. This state of affairs is called stagflation. All it means is that the consumer faces a combination of inflation and economic stagnation at the same time. When this economic condition inheres it simply means that government and the free markets are engaged in a pitched battle.

A recent illustration of government intervention for political purposes occurred during the 1980 election campaign. The United States was in the throes of a deep recession. The Federal Reserve Board established a target of 6.5 percent for money expansion. But when the summer of 1980 rolled around and the Carter administration put pressure on the Board, it gobbled up record amounts of Treasury securities, causing the money growth to explode. In June, the expansion was 15.5 percent; July 11.6 percent; August 23.9 percent; and September 16.3 percent. Arnold Moskowitz, former chief economist of Grumman Corporation and a consultant to the World Bank said that Volcker, the chairman of the Federal Reserve Board, who "has played politics, panicked by allowing excessive money expansion in the summer (which set off a new round of inflationary expectations), and now has embarked on a course that will produce a significant recession that could throw another two million people out of work."

Moskowitz went on to add: "Volcker was trying to help the re-election bid of Carter [the man who gave him his job]." (More money in circulation means more economic activity and more jobs.) And then he said: "And the panic set in when the economy began to weaken" (Dan Dorfman, columnist, *The Chicago Tribune*, Dec. 11, 1980, sec. 4, p. 9).

What happened during the summer of 1980 had its effect on the economy later that same year. By December the prime interest rate set by banks for their best customers was 20 percent. The stock market went down. A new recession was in the offing, and the new Reagan administration was to inherit a situation not of its own devising but for which the American people could hold it responsible since it would be one of the givens by the time of the inauguration. This illustration is simply another indicator of the pitched battle between government and the free market.

Nothing in America's past history suggests that government will get out of the business of intervention in economic affairs. When government continues its interference there must come a point when the recurring economic crises leave the people so prostrated that they are open to worse evils — wage and price controls, and at last the takeover of the nation either by socialism (which stands by to criticize free enterprise while the real cause of the problem is government intervention), or by some form of totalitarianism (which is also a threat to economic vitality and stability).

It is discouraging to know that the free enterprise system will be interfered with and strangulated by government intervention in the near future. It is encouraging, however, to know that the free enterprise system is resourceful and manages to fight back every time government moves forward with its interventionist program. Free market forces are always bound to curb and outwit the government as long as room for a free market economy exists. The major threat to free enterprise, then, lies in the possibility that a major economic crisis will alter the form of government and bring about a change to socialism, which will make free enterprise illegal. If and when that happens it is not the end of the battle for economic freedom.

The socialist countries are constantly confronted by what they call revisionism, and the surfacing of new sparks of bourgeois mentality, which is looked upon as a disease and a social disaster. Repression is the response to such developments in socialist countries. Any signs of a resurgent capitalist spirit must be quelled and exterminated. Western democracies do not yet seem to have grasped the truth elaborated by Solzhenitsyn in his commencement address at Harvard University in 1978 and reiterated in a statement which subsequently appeared in *Time* magazine (February 18, 1980, pp. 48, 49).

Solzhenitsyn spoke of the Soviet Union as being the subject of a lethal disease, a disease of the spirit which in physical terms takes the form of a cancer. In his diagnosis he concluded that the cancer is intractable and metastatic, that is, it affects the entire body once the disease gains a foothold, and unless radical surgery is performed the course of the disease is progressive and fatal. It is a terminal situation. Presently he perceives no possibility of the disease being stopped from within. Rather he has warned the West again and again that it is facing subjugation and perhaps annihilation by an enemy of the human spirit which has no use for humane conduct and moves ever forward in its efforts to eliminate economic freedom, and human freedom as well, for they go hand in hand. He warned the West that it, in turn, has made a commitment to materialism and consumerism which leaves out the spiritual, and that this state of affairs may guarantee victory to socialism in its war against free enterprise. While he did not say so in so many words, his thesis is consistent with the viewpoint that any capitalism based on Enlightenment presuppositions is devoid of the spiritual qualities it requires for survival.

From all of this we may gather that free market economics divorced from values inherent in the Judeo-Christian tradition is not enough. Man does not live by bread alone. There are spiritual dimensions which must accompany free enterprise, which is grounded in a market economy and which functions in accord with the laws of economics. Free enterprise, unrestrained by the Judeo-Christian value system, can ultimately be just as destructive to the human spirit as socialism, with this difference: Socialism cannot succeed, for it is not founded on good economic laws and it utterly abhors the Judeo-Christian tradition which turns out to be in opposition to the central teachings of the Enlightenment. Free enterprise may succeed, but it does not have to, and it will not, unless the social values and the human aspects of the Judeo-Christian tradition are made part and parcel of the system. When the Judeo-Christian value system is eliminated from free enterprise it will produce and it has produced a rising tide of antagonism against it in favor of socialism, which makes promises it cannot possibly fulfill.

It is of the greatest import for men to perceive that the socialist scheme which claims to be based upon the only correct historical analysis must at last enter the realm of metaphysics for which it is singularly unprepared. For once God is declared to be dead or nonexistent there is no religion, and nothing is transcendent. Thus any utopia becomes a faith promise without verifiability in history as Marx understood it. It is to this aspect of the struggle between socialism and capitalism to which we must turn for an understanding of the genius of free enterprise as we have developed it from the Old and New Testaments. But before doing so there are other matters which require our attention first.

FREEDOM AND
HUMAN RIGHTS

SOCIALISM AND FREE ENTERPRISE ARE antithetical systems which end up at variance at almost every point. As we have already learned, the question of private property ultimately lies at the root of the differences which separate the one system from the other. At the same time we must now note that freedom and human rights versus totalitarianism are also pivotal when distinguishing the characteristics which mark off free enterprise from socialism. In brief, socialism is, and must always be, marked by economic controls, by human slavery, that is, by the loss of all forms of human freedom.

Freedom and free enterprise are integrally related. The one cannot exist without the other. Freedom is an essential ingredient which goes into the making of free enterprise. But first we must define what we mean by human freedom. The hallmark of socialism is the absence of freedom and the imposition of controls at every level. The genius of laissez faire capitalism is the absence of any controls and the existence of unrestrained freedom. Socialism, no matter how much it may pay lip service to the idea of freedom, cannot continue for any length of time when freedom prevails. For freedom will always defeat socialism — which has in it intrinsically that which guarantees its demise.

We must, on the other hand, disagree with that concept of free enterprise which emphasizes individual freedom so drastically that it allows no room for any control of a substantive nature. It is here, because of man's sinfulness, that the control aspect of the Judeo-Christian world and life view must be applied to the form of free enterprise worthy of that name. Free enterprise without *any* controls becomes anarchic. What controls then must be joined to freedom to make it viable? The Hebrew-Christian tradition asserts that true freedom is grounded in the moral law of God, which moral law is asserted and defined in the Old and New Testaments. The Testaments teach that the market economy with all of its inbuilt economic laws must take into account the moral law, which can be reduced to two maxims: Love God with your whole heart and your neighbor as yourself. What does this teaching entail?

The love of neighbor, which is one of the distinctives of biblical free enterprise, can be stated both negatively and positively. Producers of goods and services will not lie, cheat, or steal. They will not envy competitors who do a better job. Nor will they be covetous. Unfair economic gimmicks such as cartels and monopolies will not be used. At the time of this writing the international oil cartel is an obvious illustration of a practice by a group of nations to rig oil prices artificially. This is possible only because these nations refuse to compete with each other, when by banding together they can force other nations to pay exorbitant prices for their oil. If nations involved in OPEC worked competitively, the price of oil would be reduced considerably. Since standards of living vary around the world and labor costs vary as well, some nations could and would sell their oil for lower prices than other nations. Pricing practices by cartels which gouge the consumer for commodities which are essential, and not luxury items, violates neighbor love. The principle of doing unto others as we would have others do unto us is the true rule of life for free enterprise based on the Judeo-Christian tradition.

Workers should be paid decent wages, however complex and difficult it is to determine what a fair wage is.
Always and ever marginal producers will go bankrupt
when wages escalate beyond their ability to remain
solvent. This in turn increases unemployment, for people
who had jobs which permitted them to live very mod-
estly now have no work at all. This severe problem
mounts when government interferes with the market
economy by setting minimum wage laws. Throughout
the history of man, certain consequences result from
minimum wage laws sooner or later. One is that when the
productivity of workers remains stable and wages keep
rising, there is a point beyond which it is impossible to
employ these people without going bankrupt. A second
effect is that labor-saving devices can be introduced,
which again produces unemployment. For example,
when labor costs rise beyond an economically profitable
level it becomes less costly to wash floors by machines
than by hand. One machine will do what four or five or
more hand workers could ordinarily do. Minimum wages
always hit the youth labor market hardest.

Young people enter the labor market with totally different gifts, inclinations, energy, vision, and persever-
ence. Some young people are always worth more to an
employer than others even though the wage rates are
the same. Employers are willing to pay better workers
larger wages, and are unhappy about paying minimum
wages to those whose productivity is lower than the
value of their wages. Moreover there is no system, including socialism, in which equality of wages ever has or
ever will exist at all levels and for all manner of skills.
Diamond cutters will always be worth more than floor
sweepers. Physicians will always be worth more than
secretaries. The more highly skilled the jobs are the
more the people are worth who perform them. And if the
educational process of preparing employees for highly
skilled jobs takes longer and is more intensive, the more

valuable the workers will be as over against those who have gone through no comparable educational regimen.

Certainly free enterprise boundaried by love of neighbor will concern itself with providing good working conditions, decent hours, and provisions for sickness, old age, and other unexpected accidents that overtake humankind. But in return for this, employers have every right to expect their employees to do their jobs with dispatch. Loafing, shoddy workmanship, and indifference on the part of wage earners are just as much a denial of the law of neighbor love as the failure of employers to fulfill their moral obligations. Moreover, both employers and employees have a responsibility to see that the consumer gets a decent product in working order and with the expectancy that it will last him for a reasonable length of time.

Given the nature of life, the needs of men, and the demands of society, there never will be completely safe business operations with no human risks entailed. Coal mining, for example, is an enterprise laden with physical risks for employees. Black lung disease abounds. Working underground is dangerous and cave-ins do occur. But coal is a necessary product and has been for hundreds and hundreds of years. When employers have done as much as they can (and many do not do this) to ensure the welfare of their employees, it will never be enough to eliminate all of the risks inherent in such operations. The same situation exists in multitudes of business enterprises. Workmen who accept dangerous assignments do so with the knowledge of the risks involved. Employers also know of these risks. But these are some of the hard facts of life, and until the millennium arrives it will always be like this.

One of the great problems faced by free enterprise comes from international trade operations when there are no tariff barriers to prevent import and export relations between nations. A nation in which free enterprise controlled by the love of neighbor principle exists is at a disadvantage when trade relations are established with other nations which either do not have free enterprise or which do have it but refuse to include the restraints imposed on it by the Judeo-Christian tradition of neighbor love. Unfortunately the Judeo-Christian tradition does not exist in large measure around the world. It certainly does not exist, nor are its principles applied, in the socialist nations of the world. And some of the other nations which are not yet socialist also do not hold to neighbor love the way we are talking about it here. As a result, sweat shops abound, labor is paid a barely livable wage, and products derived from this underpaid labor can flood the markets of nations bound by the tradition of which we are speaking. This form of competition constitutes a real problem for any employer, and all workers, and is a challenge as well as a threat to existing enterprises. The challenge is to increase the productivity of better paid labor so as to make the business competitive. The threat is that of being forced to go out of that particular business with resultant unemployment and a failure to create wealth in the nation where this takes place. The people who profit from this situation are the importers and exporters who as middlemen have the opportunity to make money.

The world economic situation is complex and true justice ever remains elusive. Justice may obtain here and there, but full justice for all people will always be an unreached goal somewhere, with an unchanging agenda to work for it until time as we know it shall be no more. What then is the conclusion of the matter about freedom? Freedom, under a system of free enterprise guarded by the law of neighbor love, is man's most precious possession. It belongs to man inherently because he is man. It derives from the Creator who made him and has given to all men his creation ordinances of which human freedom is a basic component. Creation did not intend servitude for man. He was to be free to choose and to live a life of freedom in which he *could* make his own choices. He could sit on the earth and starve to death if he so chose. And having made this choice it was *not* the responsibility of other men to feed him who refused to work. Or he could choose where to work, what work to do, when to do it, and how much of his time and energy should be spent in doing it. If he could labor five hours a week and produce enough to survive and to satisfy his own estimate of his needs and of his expectations from life, that would be his free choice.

True freedom includes the right to do, or not to do. It includes the right to starve or to become affluent. It includes the right for man to determine his own life style, to spend and keep, or to give away what he has as he chooses. This same freedom includes the right to labor under the mandate of the law of neighbor love or not to do so. He may opt for socialism or for free enterprise. But he should know or will learn that socialism is a utopian dream, an economic system which because of man's nature will fail. He should also know or will learn that free enterprise without the restraint of neighbor love is still superior to socialism in meeting man's material needs because it takes into account the nature of man. It was formulated for man as he is, not man as we would like to see him be. The survival of socialism depends upon the development of the "new man" who nowhere can be found or will be found. On the other hand free enterprise will do for man by way of meeting his material needs what socialism cannot do. Free enterprise can and will do this for a long period of time without the law of love, but if its freedom is moderated by neighbor love it will do so indefinitely. The choice is man's.

ECONOMIC FREEDOM

The loss of economic freedom is one of the first results of turning to socialism. Its loss is incalculable. Socialism has for its first economic principle the abolition of the right to private property. Once this is gone little is left for the people except involuntary servitude, no matter how exaltingly the masters describe the glories of working for the motherland. Once private property is done away with, all of the means of production are owned by the state. This is true despite the patently false claim that everything belongs to the people. It turns out that when everybody owns everything, nobody owns anything. Community ownership is a fiction at best, an appalling misrepresentation at worst.

Farms are state owned and farmers are tied to the land. In the Soviet Union the loss of farm ownership by the farmers was so economically destructive that the state was finally forced to allow each farmer to use an acre of land whatever purpose he wished. The agricultural production on those few acres and the "privilege" of selling what the users produce in an open market manner reveals how badly state ownership of farms works. This procedure is a concession to free enterprise and is a prostitution of theoretical socialism and a pragmatic approach to an otherwise insoluble problem.

Workers must stay where they are placed by their rulers. Changing jobs is hazardous. Factory production is inefficient. The products are sleezy. Soviet citizens buy imports from other countries whenever they can. There is no incentive for workers to increase their productivity. If they do this, the bureaucrats increase their monthly production quotas without raising their wages. It doesn't take long for laborers to realize that the system works against their personal interests. Consequently they do as little work as possible and they take no pride in what they do. It is customary for them to do most of the work the last third of the month to meet their quotas. And the consumers are smart enough to know that it is bad policy to buy anything rushed through the factory system the last third of any month. The goods are often hardly worth buying.

The bureaucrats make the decisions as to what will be produced and how much. But the consumer is still, in some measure, king. Warehouses fill up with items the consumers refuse to buy. If only badly produced articles are available, the consumer gets caught short. Prices are fixed by the state so there are no sales or bargains. Advertising about available goods is in short supply. Consumers never know in advance what will be in stock at the stores. When something worthwhile, and often in short supply, becomes available, friends and relatives are advised immediately and the stock disappears from the shelves quickly.

In order to keep its citizens on the farms (which function so badly that the Soviet Union is increasingly dependent on Western agricultural production), farmers are not free to migrate to the big cities. In order for anyone to live in Moscow he must secure a pass to do so. Apartments are in short supply and waiting lists are long. Multifamily people occupy three-room flats when they do live in the city. Moving from one flat to another when the size of the family increases is a yeoman feat for inventive and calculating minds.

Substantial illicit, underground economic activity goes on unabated. People quickly learn how to beat the system. Thievery is commonplace and inventories disappear without anyone knowing where they have gone to. Corruption abounds and bribery is so commonplace in order for consumers to obtain what they need that it is impossible for the authorities, many of whom are engaged in similar activities for their personal benefit, to eliminate them.

Stores are owned and operated by the state. But there are stores and stores. The average citizen buys from state stores on the lowest level. Other stores which stock higher quality goods can be entered only by those who are in the upper structures of Soviet society. The leaders, according to the stratum to which one belongs, enjoy the good life at the expense of the common masses. The classless society is a myth and the promise of it in the future is an unrealized and unrealizable dream. Foreign goods of excellent quality are available in these special stores. The prices are right (that is, subsidized) so that it is safe to say that it is not how much you earn that counts; it is how much you can get for what you earn. The elite get more for their money than do any in the other strata of society.

The economic gap between the lowest and highest paid people in the Soviet Union is greater than in the capitalist countries (which are so constantly the object of Soviet criticism for their supposed injustice and their unconcern for the masses). The hypocrisy of the socialist system defies imagination, but a true picture has been painted graphically by Hedrick Smith in his outstanding book illuminating Soviet life, entitled *Russia*.

The worst predicament of all prevails for the man caught up in the tentacles of the law, or who is suspected of "crime" by the KGB, or who is known for his dissent. He can be fired. And if and when he finds other work, the omnipresent police apparatus catches up with him, and he is again unemployed and becomes dependent on friends, if he has any, to keep body and soul together. Some people caught up in this skein of persecution do obtain minor and low-paying jobs, performing work far beneath their gifts and capacities. But they have been so beaten down by the system and its inherent injustice that they can do no more than exist while they live out unfilled and unrewarding lives under a tyranny totally destructive of freedom and devoid of human rights of any kind. Moreover, disemployed people are regarded as parasites and can be imprisoned.

On the economic side, workers cannot strike to improve their material condition. The very notion of a strike is contrary to the basic theory of socialism. Since the workers, in theory, own everything, it is considered impossible for them to strike against themselves. If and when strikes are threatened or do occur they are automatically said to be a deviation from the "true faith," a sign of bourgeois mentality which is regarded as heretical and automatically to be quelled. Curiously, if the workers are really the owners of the factories it is difficult to see how the omnipresent state can indict them for any transgression, since the peoples' democracy is held up as the ideal. If the workers are their own masters, how can they be wrong unless they are rejecting what they are already supposed to have accepted in principle?

The situation in Poland in the fall of 1980 poignantly pointed up the Achilles' heel of socialism. The workers decided to strike for higher wages, shorter hours, and better representation in the government. The communist-dominated leadership, prodded by the Soviet Union, appealed to the workers not to strike and to accept the longer working week because of the economic problems of the nation. This was an appeal to their patriotism. Apparently the workers saw clearly that the system which promised them economic utopia was incapable of, or opposed to, fulfilling its promises. Dialectical materialism may feed the mind but it can hardly fill empty bellies. What the workers may not yet have grasped is the undeniable fact that it is the Western "capitalistic and imperialistic" world which has enabled Poland to avoid complete economic disaster. Were it not for the financing of the Polish state by Western capital through loans which may never be repaid, the economic plight of the Polish people would have been infinitely worse than it was by the end of 1980.

The Polish situation was worsened considerably by the massed armies of the Russian bear which surround this unfortunate nation on all sides. The Soviet Union stated as plainly as possible that if necessary it would intervene militarily in Poland to preserve socialism. This threat, of course, is part of the Brezhnev doctrine that wherever and whenever a socialist state is in danger of being subverted by reactionary anti-socialist propaganda, it is the intention of the Soviet Union to meet the threat with military force. In other words the people, that is, the proletariat, are not free to change the existing system even if they desire to do so. Their proletarian democracy turns out to be a fiction. Dissidence, even when it involves the great majority of the workers, is not allowable, for it represents a denial of socialist principles. And this cannot be tolerated. This sort of democracy turns out to be just another totalitarianism, and behind the totalitarian reality stands the non-democratic, imperialistic, world-dominating Soviet Union.

The Polish people are free to do what they please so long as it is in accord with Soviet wishes. Every deviation from traditional socialist viewpoints is looked upon as planned and executed by the Western capitalists. Deviation is perceived as part of the dialectic process in which socialism and imperialism are engaged in a titanic struggle for world domination. But the communists are assured of their ultimate triumph by their peculiar philosophy of history. This is the "rabbit in the hat" of socialism which has no foundation in history and is no more than a "faith" premise based on no other authority than the visionary imagination of the founders of the socialist "religion." Fortunately for the world, time is beginning to demonstrate inexorably that socialism is founded on mythology and simply will not produce what it promises. This knowledge, however, has not yet been grasped by the underdeveloped nations who have been led to believe that their problems are the consequence of imperialistic capitalism whereas, in reality, their downtrodden condition stems from the lack of free enterprise, not the employment of it.

The absence of economic freedom lies at the heart of the world's failure to provide the goods and services they so desperately need and want. But along with the absence of economic freedom there goes the loss of other freedoms which are no less essential to true human rights. The second victim of socialism is the loss of religious freedom.

RELIGIOUS FREEDOM

Nowhere in the world where socialism holds sway does genuine freedom of religion prevail. Religion, whether it be Christianity, or even such ethnic religions as Buddhism, Hinduism, Islam, or others, is a victim of socialist thought. Soviet Marxism and all of its varieties including that of the People's Republic of China, is a deadly enemy of religious freedom. Whether we like it or not, religious beliefs stand opposed to historical materialism. The acceptance of Marxist socialism makes impossible the true viability of religious freedom.

Numbers of thinkers including the promoters of the theology of liberation in Latin America, act, talk, or write as though it is possible to accept the Marxist vision of the historical processes and cling to the Judeo-Christian tradition at the same time. Such people must be suspect as far as their religious faith and commitment are concerned. Many of them may well be crypto-Christians and hard-line Marxists. Others may be simply ignorant or intellectually muddled. Whatever the state of their minds, they are opposed to free enterprise. And if and when they gain control of any state it will soon become necessary for them to choose between Marxism's antagonism to all religion and their theoretical commitment to the Judeo-Christian world and life view. Experience teaches that when this happens they opt for Marxism and their religious fervor evaporates.

It is true that some Marxist states pay lip service to religious freedom but in practice these states eliminate all religion from the schools, teach atheism at all times, and otherwise belittle, degrade, and make light of religious faith. There is no Marxist state where any leader of any importance is a known adherent, proponent, or propagator of the Judeo-Christian faith. Religious belief is the surest guarantee that opportunities at all levels of economic and political life under socialism will be forbidden territory for the believer. In the Soviet Union thousands of church buildings have become museums. Whatever theological education exists is under the strictest surveillance by the state and by the security agencies. Clergymen who say anything unfavorable to the Marxist enterprise are either removed from their posts and placed in regions where they can do the least damage or they are sent to Siberia.

It is not without good reason that the claim has been made that the Russian Orthodox Church, which is a member of the World Council of Churches, has been infiltrated by the KGB and can do nothing of importance without the government's consent and approval. At the fifth plenum of the World Council of Churches in Nairobi a few years ago a motion was made and passed which was critical of the Soviet Union. Other motions were passed which were far more critical of South Korea, South Africa, and Rhodesia (Zimbabwe). The Russian Orthodox representatives reacted strongly and immediately against the action of the majority of the Assembly regarding the Soviet Union. By devious and questionable means the issue was resurfaced and the WCC leadership nullified the action and agreed instead to have a meeting later the same day to consider the situation. Meanwhile the Orthodox delegates, under the obvious eyes of the KGB agents, who were omnipresent, threatened that the church would leave the World Council if the action stood as originally voted. Needless to say, the motions critical of the non-Marxist nations were not withdrawn. The motion which was critical of the Soviet Union, however, was reversed and nothing similar to the condemnations of South Korea and South Africa was said about a nation which has been and is far more of a transgressor of religious principles than the other states that were excoriated.

It is true that some degree of religious *toleration* is allowed in the various Marxist states. But religious *freedom* exists nowhere and is not likely to become a reality so long as socialism remains in power anywhere. Toleration is not enough, for what is at stake is the right to religious freedom which cannot be bargained away and which stands everywhere among men as one of the natural rights written large in the universe itself. Wherever and whenever men are forced to believe or not to believe, religious freedom is dead. When men like Georgi Vins in the Soviet Union can be sentenced to Siberia for Baptist convictions, religious freedom is imperiled. When parents are forbidden to teach religion to their children and when children from religious homes are studiously inculcated with atheistic teachings, religious freedom is negated.

It should come as no surprise to anyone why religious freedom is always a victim of socialism. Religious faith presents socialism with one of its most serious challenges. The Marxist view that religion is a product of bourgeois thinking, an invention designed to keep the proletariat under the thumb of the bourgeoisie, is virtually omnipresent in Marxist thinking. Religion is the opiate of the people, an enemy of the Marxist ideology, and will overthrow socialism if it ever gets powerful enough to do so. Thus religion is not an option for socialism by which those who are religious and those who are atheists can live side by side in peace and harmony. Marxism cannot afford the luxury of whatever competes with its system. Thus religion is an ever-present enemy and a genuine threat to the socialist system and its theoretical foundations.

When mainland China was overtaken by the Marxists, missionary outreach and the Christian faith were among the first victims. Taiwan, on the other hand, was, is, and will remain an open door to missionary activity. Missionaries are not allowed to enter mainland China, or the Soviet Union, or North Korea, and some who were imprisoned by Castro's Marxist Cuba have only recently been released from their servitude. The Muslim nations of the Middle East are beginning to understand the threat of socialism to their religious faith. Yet Marxism has made inroads into these nations and is working sedulously to turn them into the same kind of totalitarian state that the Soviet Union presently is.

The Christian faith is especially offensive to the Marxist mind. At the heart of Protestantism lies the notion of the priesthood of all believers. This leads a man to accept his manhood in all of its fullness, and confers on him a dignity missing in socialism. The Christian man is something and somebody. His goals and his aims are different. He wants to glorify God, not the state. He holds to a system of ethics which countermands virtually all of the Marxist ethical principles. He exhibits love which puts God first, his neighbor second, and himself last. This is totally foreign to Marxist thinking. It regards religion as an aberration inbuilt in bourgeois thinking.

Religious freedom is only one of the freedoms for the Christian man. Alongside his religious freedom is the freedom of his person to go where he wishes to go and live where he is pleased to live, about which we shall say more shortly. Moreover, he becomes infused with the biblical endorsement of private property, the right to think as he pleases, and the notion that political freedom includes the right to express his own opinion freely even though it runs counter to the majority mindset. Moreover, he cannot and will not be bound in his conscience by any system which defies the basic principles of his faith, particularly a system which allows for only one party and condemns political dissent.

The Christian cannot help being a nuisance to the Marxist mentality, a termite who will bring about the collapse of the socialist system. There is every reason for the Marxist to be paranoid about the Christian faith and other faiths as well. But this is not all. Socialism hates with a vengeance what we might call the freedom of the mind.

FREEDOM OF THE MIND

The freedom of the mind is another victim of socialism. Socialism is confident that all men should think the same way and come to the same conclusions. There is only one way to think and that is the socialist way. Any other way of thinking is automatically classified as being bourgeois based. Since bourgeois thinking is wrong thinking, it cannot be allowed, and wherever it sprouts it must be killed off. The only freedom to think is to think the socialist way. Any other kind of thought is dangerous to the state and especially to the one who thinks differently, for he must be "cured" by brainwashing, the Siberia treatment, mental hospital confinement, or death. Differences of opinion cannot be allowed to persist lest they bring about changes which will threaten the socialist state.

There is a sense in which it is possible for someone to think non-socialist thoughts. So long as he keeps them to himself and does nothing about them there is no problem for the state, only a problem for the tortured soul who entertains thoughts he can never share with other people in any overt form. If he does, he becomes the object of special attention by the authorities, who use a variety of means to silence him effectively. But of what value is thought which cannot be expressed? And where is there freedom if a man can only think what is already laid out for him in advance and from which he cannot dissent? The genius of thinking is the right to examine all systems of thought; to bring them under the scrutiny of the thinker who may think new thoughts, or change old ones; or to challenge current thinking rigorously to see whether it stands the test of argumentation and debate. Since asking a question about the socialist philosophy is assumed to be a deviation from the system, no questions can be asked without dangerous consequences.

Good thinkers normally will write down their thoughts. And best of all, thinkers hope to have their thoughts incorporated in book form for others to read. In socialist countries there are no book publishers except the state itself. There is a board of review which approves all manuscripts before publication. Nothing of a contradictory nature which calls into question anything about the socialist system is permitted to be published. How many books will be made available to the public and how the books will be distributed is decided by the state. Freedom of the press or freedom of publication is nonexistent in socialist paradises. Therefore people are fed only what their masters want them to read. The highly esteemed democracy of the proletariat turns out to be the tightest kind of thought control and censorship the world has ever known.

Those who think are usually clever enough to beat the system so that their literary productions can see the light of day. One method is to distribute literature surreptitiously or undercover. Copies are passed from person to person in unprinted form and make their influence felt among those who have access to this form of distribution. Sometimes authors smuggle their manuscripts out of the Soviet Union to the free world where their books can be published—but not for the people of their home country, unless they get their books back into the country illicitly.

It is next to impossible for people from the free world to understand and appreciate what a free press means until they live in socialist countries where a free press does not exist. Book buyers cannot purchase or read what is not available. And only that which the state thinks people should read is distributed. It is not what people want but what they are allowed to buy that characterizes socialism. It is no wonder then that a nation like the Soviet Union can maintain its hegemony over its captive millions, since they are not allowed to peek behind the dark curtain of another world of which they have little awareness. Free speech, freely available books of every sort, and a truly free newspaper press would bring socialism down in a short period of time, if this freedom existed. But it does not, and it will not be allowed the innocent victims of totalitarianism, which has for its first and only purpose the continuance of its control over the masses of its people.

There is one method of acquainting the people of the Soviet Union and Red China with what is happening around the world and what people are thinking. This instrument is radio, particularly of the short wave variety. As long as people have radios they can listen to broadcasts from the free world. So dangerous does the Soviet Union regard radio broadcasts emanating from the free world that the Soviet masters jam the air waves to keep the people from listening to these programs. The people of Red China, given the physical size of that nation, and the fact that there are fewer radio transmitters to blanket the country, are less likely to hear about what is happening outside the nation itself.

In all socialist nations, newspapers are available to the

people. One of the first acts of a newly installed socialist regime in any nation is to take over control of the press. Then, only that is printed which the socialist leadership wants its people to know. But even if the press were to be free for a season, it might not bring down the socialist system. The armed forces of every socialist nation are usually powerful enough to prevent uprisings among the people. And the suppression of a free press takes place.

The socialist answer to freedom of thought and speech is repression. The latest reports coming from the Soviet Union indicate that the most recent surge toward freedom of speech represented by the works and activities of people like Aleksandr Solzhenitsyn are being slowly but surely controlled by the forces of socialist repression. Hundreds of victims have been arrested and shipped off to Siberia, or to prison, or to mental hospitals. These dissidents, for that is what they are called, are relatively few in number, courageous of heart, bright of mind, and determined of spirit. Somehow they manage to keep the light of free speech flickering. They hope that someday it will become a flaming fire which will liberate them from their mental straitjackets and enable them once again to be free men and women who can think as they wish, write what they have to say, and make their product available to all who freely and of their own choice wish to read their words.

If anyone needs further confirmation about how socialism reacts to freedom of speech and of the press once it gains control of a country, a look at what happened in Nicaragua in 1980 should provide the answer. Surely no one would claim that Anastasio Somoza, the former president who was later murdered, was an ideal democratic leader whose policies should have been endorsed or followed. But Somoza at his worst was better than the socialist option under the Sandinista rebels who are ardent Marxists.

From the beginning of Jimmy Carter's presidency he

was determined to see that Somoza was overthrown, even though he had been a friend of the United States. Mr. Carter used his extensive powers to tighten the screws on Somoza and Nicaragua so as to guarantee it would fall into the hands of the communists. Pressure was placed on the International Monetary Fund to block badly needed credit for Nicaragua on two occasions. President Carter instructed the U.S. Department of Agriculture to shut down beef exports to the United States from Nicaragua. Ambassador William Bowdler told Somoza that "the Carter policy was to see that all of the right-wing governments in Central America were replaced and that Nicaragua would be the first to go."

The Sandinista rebels were financed by Cuba and trained there. Once the Somoza regime was overthrown and the Sandinistas took over, they followed the logical pattern of socialism—freedom of speech and the freedom of the press were eliminated. One writer said: ". . . the human rights campaign was the human bloodshed campaign. That instrument of Mr. Carter's was responsible for deaths of thousands of people. And what do they now have in Nicaragua? After the Marxist victory, thousands of innocent people were slaughtered, and this mayhem continues to this very day. The people of Nicaragua now have no rights at all. The jails are full of political prisoners who have committed no crime" (America's Future, Vol. 22, No. 23, November 28, 1980, p. 6).

Once again the record speaks for itself. Socialism will lose out in a free society. Thus it must always remove every vestige of freedom, not the least of which is the freedom of speech and of the press. Nicaragua now is a Marxist socialist state with little reason to suppose that it can be delivered from its bondage by peaceful means. Only a revolution will make this change possible.

At the time of this writing the same thing that transpired in Nicaragua is happening in El Salvador. The leftists in that country have been carrying on guerrilla warfare there for many months. Early in January of 1981 the Marxists announced what they described as their "final offensive" against the junta. The Farabundo Marti National Liberation Front, a federation of five or six leftist guerrilla groups, were waging war against the military-civilian junta, that is, the forces opposed to Marxism. The guerrillas sought by every means to intimidate the people of El Salvador and to get the soldiers of the legitimate government to desert and to join the leftists in what they described as their "fight against the Christian Democratic dictatorship." What they failed to say was that they had another kind of dictatorship in mind which, if they succeeded in overthrowing the government, would be far more oppressive and would carry out totalitarianism, to the nth degree. They would move immediately to take over the means of communication, that is, radio, TV, and the newspapers. From that moment on the people would get only what their masters wanted them to see and hear and read.

It is important to note here that the Judeo-Christian tradition freely guarantees to others what it demands for itself by way of free speech. Thus those who vigorously oppose the Judeo-Christian tradition have every right to do so and to make their dissent known wherever, whenever, and however they choose. If coercion were applied to deny freedom of speech to those who reject the foundational principles of the Judeo-Christian tradition the day would soon dawn when freedom of speech for those who accept the Judeo-Christian tradition would be lost as well. True freedom of speech also applies to the man with whom I have the profoundest disagreement. He has the right to say what he wants without being silenced, threatened, or imprisoned. Otherwise there is no freedom of speech. And if freedom of speech means only the right to accept what I hold to be true, then it is no longer freedom. Defenders of freedom of speech are caught up in the dilemma of how to respond to those who demand freedom of speech, ironically, to attain their objective of *destroying* that freedom after they gain control.

FREEDOM OF PERSON

Another victim of socialist philosophy is the loss of personal freedom. This includes the right to leave the country, that is, to denationalize oneself to become a citizen of another nation. Thousands of Jews in the Soviet Union have fought to leave to go to Israel or other Western nations. Multiplied numbers of them have not succeeded in obtaining permission to do so. The option of leaving one nation for another is a human right which no government can justifiably disallow. But the socialist states care little about this. The recent exception, when Fidel Castro released thousands of Cubans to go to America, does not represent a change of attitude. He had ulterior motives in mind, one of which was to embarrass the United States by exporting criminals, mentally ill citizens, and no doubt a contingent of secret agents of the government, who will later prove to be a problem for the United States.

Freedom of personhood includes the right to live any place a citizen of a nation desires to go. Socialist countries restrict citizens' freedom by means of permits which assign them to a location from which they cannot move without security permission. One of the worst cases of oppression in 1980 involved Andrei Sakharov, the 1965 Nobel Peace Prize laureate, an active dissident who publicly opposed Soviet repression and who was a friend and supporter of Aleksandr Solzhenitsyn. Sakharov was placed under house arrest. He was exiled to Gorky, a gray provincial city three hundred miles east of Moscow. His telephone was disconnected and he was allowed no visitors except his wife.

Solzhenitsyn is another case in point. He had no intention whatever of leaving his native land. He wished to speak out in opposition to the awful repression. In his case the Soviet Union expatriated him. His expulsion was not by his request or desire. It was simply the best way for the Soviets to rid themselves of a worldwide notable whom they could not consign to Siberia again, or place in a psychiatric ward, or execute. The attention of the world was fixed on the Solzhenitsyn case, and this fact alone probably saved his life. He *was* guilty of anti-Soviet activity, which in their parlance means he was not a faithful advocate of the socialist system. Instead he openly and widely criticized that system. His writings were eagerly read around the world and brought him international acclaim in literature.

Freedom of personhood is denied Soviet citizens in their work occupations. The state can keep a person where it wants him to be. If someone leaves his job and does not find another one he is subject to arrest for being a societal parasite. And this can be accomplished, as we have already said, by the security forces getting someone fired from his job and preventing him from securing other employment. After that he is arrested for being a parasite. This opens the door to a trip to prison or to Siberia, from whence few prisoners return to a normal life.

Travel is closely regulated in socialist countries. Police checks on travelers are commonplace. And if there is no good reason for someone to be where he is, the police power is employed to keep such a person from staying where he might become dangerous to the state. In any dictatorship the freedom of movement by the citizenry is a human right which is quickly curtailed. It is indisputable that such freedom is dangerous even in democracies.

It makes possible the rapid and legal movement from one place to another with ease and without interruption. Terrorists, anarchists, and revolutionaries in countries like the United States use this human right to strike against "the system," that is, against free enterprise, in an endeavor to create revolutionary conditions which may lead to the overthrow of the existing system and its replacement by socialism.

Democracies are always tempted to respond to anarchic conditions by adopting policies similar to those found in socialist countries. When democracies do this they are resorting to a deprivation of human rights, a state of affairs they denounce in socialist countries. The philosophic problem is that the freedom of persons is denied in order to protect the freedom of persons! Yet a nation like the United States has written into its legal system the right of the state to protect itself by declaring martial law, establishing curfews, and the like. There can be no doubt that martial law is a legitimate and effective tool to prevent the destruction of the government, and its use should be encouraged so long as it is employed for a limited time until the danger is past. It is either martial law or anarchy, and the former is preferable. Obviously the temporary restriction of human rights may leave a nation open to a dictatorship of the right, as a countermeasure against the efforts of the left to bring the government down. But there seems to be no way to avoid this dilemma.

The socialist countries regard any effort directed against socialism as counterrevolutionary, and such activities, whether they involve freedom of person or any other freedom, are forbidden. So when a democracy is under attack and its existence is threatened by socialist forces, the lesser of two evils is to use martial law to prevent the destruction of democracy. This is *not* a denial of human freedom but a temporary interruption of it until pacific conditions return.

POLITICAL FREEDOM

The last of the human freedoms and what surely is one of the most important of all freedoms is that of political dissent. At its heart it implies the right and indeed the necessity for the citizenry to organize itself into competing political enclaves. It may be a two-party system or a multi-party system. This is the democratic approach and offers maximum freedom for people to convince other people of the rightness of their views and to vote for their candidates for public office.

A two-party or multi-party system is anathema to socialism. It knows of only one party, for socialism is caught up in its class struggle concept which, while it is essentially related to the political, spills over into other freedoms as well. The essence of the class struggle concept, which is the centerpiece of the Marxist or socialist philosophy of history, is the notion that above the primitive level all societies are split into two classes and only two classes. And these two classes are engaged in a titanic struggle. This, they claim, is the basic reality of all social relationships everywhere around the globe. The two classes are the bourgeoisie and the proletariat.

The dogma of the class struggle was never defined by Karl Marx. Indeed it was constructed out of fancy, not out of fact, and had to be accepted by faith. Basically Marx concluded that all people ultimately can be identified with one of two classes. The bourgeoisie control the means of the production. The proletariat do not. Between them there must be, and inevitably will be, profound opposition. It is through the class struggle that progress is made and it is in this connection that the terms thesis, antithesis, and synthesis are used. The claim is made that what lies behind history is not war between nations, the clash of national interest, or anything else other than the clash between classes or the class struggle. The two classes into which all men are divided are not common to one society but to all societies. And each class is not limited to itself in a given nation, for the property owners of all nations belong to the same class and the workers of all countries belong to the other class. In other words, the entire world is divided into two classes. And the sole element which separates one class from the other is private property.

Throughout history a warfare has been going on in which the existing bourgeois class, the thesis, is challenged by the proletariat, the antithesis, and rising out of that conflict there comes into being a synthesis. The synthesis in turn becomes the new thesis and is challenged by an antithesis, out of which struggle the new synthesis emerges. Marxism claims that modern capitalism, which has evolved into imperialism, is the last thesis which is being challenged by Marxism. Marxism will then lead to socialism, which will become communism and the fight will be over. The proletariat, that is, the working class, must win according to Marx's theory.

At the heart of the politics of Marxism lies the abolition of private property. The theory is that when private property is eradicated, since it is the cause of the class struggle, the utopia men dream of will become a reality. It is interesting that Marxism supposes that the bourgeoisie and the proletarians think as they do because of their class status. Both classes must think the way they do. In other words, a proletarian cannot think like the bourgeoisie. And vice versa. The meaning of this must be made plain. In the present or final battle the bourgeoisie must lose. The proletarians must win. When the bourgeoisie have been disposed of there will be only proletarians. Of necessity they must think alike. Since this is so, there is no need for more than one party. Everybody will think like a proletarian and nobody like a bourgeois person. Any member of the proletariat who thinks differently from what a proletarian should think is automatically labeled a bourgeois mentality and dealt with. For anyone to suppose that there can be a second political party in the Soviet Union with different objectives from the Communist Party is to think like a bourgeoisie, and this is forbidden. Thus there is and there can be no political freedom in socialist countries.

Until the socialist state comes into being, there is room for more than one political party in every nation. In the United States this means there are the Republican and Democratic parties. But there is also the Communist Party. It presently has a legal right to exist in this democracy even though it has for its chief objective the overthrow of the present political system. The genius of democracy lies in its multi-party principle. The election of 1980 provided an interesting example of how the two-party system gave way to a three-party presidential election. It is true that the Communist Party had no chance of electing a president. But Mr. Carter and Mr. Reagan were opposed by Congressman Anderson of Illinois. When he was unable to secure the Republican nomination, he pulled out of the party and ran as an independent. Only in a democracy would this be a possibility.

In socialist countries the slate of candidates for office must be members of the Communist Party. Only one candidate appears on the ballot for each office. The political freedom of the voter is limited to voting for or against one candidate. Needless to say, most candidates are elected by virtually 100 percent of the vote. At best the number of votes cast against any given candidate is never more than 1 or 2 percent. And if those who registered their dissent were known, it would work against them in their daily lives. Freedom, to be freedom, must produce its own fruit, and that means no fewer than two parties in any political election. And the selection process to determine which candidates will run for each party is arrived at democratically, not by party assignment and decision.

Perhaps it is most fitting to say that the political principle employed by socialists everywhere is this: "When I am weaker, I ask you for liberty because that is *your* principle; but when I am stronger, I take it away from you because it is *not* my principle."

SUMMATION

Human freedoms are cut out of one piece of cloth. Either they exist or they don't. The various freedoms are indivisible. If one is lost the others will be discarded as well. This can be illustrated by religious freedom. Every religion has a world and life view. That view includes all aspects of life—economic, political, social, personal, and mental. Of what use is religious freedom if my religious views in political, social, and economic matters are not also sacrosanct? If my world and life view calls for the validation of private property and that freedom is gone, of what use is my religious freedom (for it is being abridged)? When my religious view of life includes the right to free speech, of what value is my religious viewpoint when freedom of speech is taken from me? If my religious convictions make it impossible for me to vote for a candidate, but there is only one candidate and no possibility of having other candidates on the ballot who hold an opposing view, of what value is my religious freedom when it cannot be freely exercised in the political realm?

Freedom and democracy go hand in hand. It is true that democracy is not a particularly good form of government, but every other alternative is worse. Freedom is loaded with dangers, but it is better than slavery and at least opens up the possibility that men may choose to live together in peace. The only alternative to freedom and democracy is totalitarianism, in which the few hold sway over the great majority of the people. Totalitarianism is contrary to nature and to the knowledge of God in the Judeo-Christian tradition. The liberation of the Israelites from their bondage to Pharaoh in Egypt forever stands as a great symbol of man's never-ending quest for freedom. But whatever bondage men may experience, any liberation from that bondage by the substitution of socialism, at best, can only mean a worse form of slavery. But when men can be delivered from their bondage, whatever it may consist in, and when free enterprise with all of its human freedoms is put in its place, then there is the certainty that man's material needs will be cared for better than by any other system. And the existence of freedom will open the door to the opportunity to embrace the Judeo-Christian tradition, which gives free enterprise a human face and counters man's as yet unperfected and unperfectable human nature in this life. Freedom makes possible the undergirding of free enterprise with an altruism which has for its cardinal tenet the second table of the Law—to love my neighbor as I love myself.

Those who believe in free enterprise and democracy should never forget that their freedom and their economic convictions may need to be defended in a variety of ways against enemies of those freedoms within and without. In an ideal world this would not become a necessity. Men of good will could disagree about the validity of one economic system over another. And they would be willing to test one over the other by human experience. But when the issue is human freedom versus bondage and human slavery, there is no room for testing the one against the other. This has been made clear in the Polish crisis of early 1981.

Both the Polish Communist leaders and the Soviet Union have shouted loudly and forcefully that the people of Poland are not free to change their system from that of totalitarianism to democracy. Nor are they free to replace economic socialism with free enterprise. Nor can the Communists allow the workers freedom to disagree with or change things, even though they mouth the slogan that socialism is truly representative of the workers and that the workers own the means of production. The desire of workers to change their economic circumstances is labeled "aggression." It is anti-socialistic and reactionary. It is opposed to the "struggle of the peoples for their national, economic, and social emancipation." It constitutes an act of hostility against the socialist forces. It cannot be permitted to continue. It must be stopped, whatever the cost.

When the Western democracies face this kind of mentality, a mentality which openly declares that its purpose is to destroy democracy and eliminate free enterprise around the globe, there is only one course of action they can pursue. They must resist this threat at every point and must consider that one of the options is armed conflict. Tens of thousands of the peoples from Cambodia, Vietnam, China, and the Soviet Union itself lie dead because they refused to buy the socialist way of life; they were exterminated. The statement of the Red Dean of the English Anglican Church years ago that it is "better to be Red than dead" is not one that honest men who cherish freedom can accept. There are times when death is to be preferred to other alternatives. It is better to die for freedom than it is to live a slave. It is quite consistent with the Judeo-Christian tradition to be willing to die for what those in that tradition believe.

The question may well be asked: If the Communists are willing to die for what they profess to believe, why should not those who believe in freedom and free enterprise be willing to do the same? That which is not worth defending to the death is not something to live by in any event. In the case of the United States there are enemies within who seek to destroy America's human freedoms and its economic way of life. These enemies use their freedom in this democracy to advocate the taking away of our freedom after they gain control. They are not the workers. They most frequently are among the intelligentsia and the affluent. For those who adhere to the Judeo-Christian tradition the issue is self-evident. The two crucial issues which mark off socialism from the Judeo-Christian tradition are these: The inalienability of private property which has to do with the economic realm, and the right to human freedoms such as we have explicated here. People who hold to the Judeo-Christian tradition and those who may hold to that tradition without an understanding of its soteriological aspects must make their choice: human freedom and free enterprise or slavery and state ownership of the means of production.

Which will it be?

SOCIALIST ETHICS
AND MORALITY

SOCIALIST ETHICS AND MORALITY MUST BE looked at and compared with those of the Judeo-Christian tradition, and indeed, with the tradition to be found in all of the ethnic religions. When this is done it will be seen that socialist ethics and morality are strongly opposed to all the underlying principles of religion and particularly of the Judeo-Christian faith.

SOCIALISM AND CREEDALISM

Socialism has its own religion, despite Marx's denial of all religion and his assumption that it springs from the minds of men and is an expression of class consciousness. Socialism holds that we live in a world that is doomed because of its internal contradictions. Yet it promises that from the death of the old world a new and beautiful one will emerge, based upon the advent of the new man. At that time all men will live together in peace and plenty. But this vision is not in any sense transcendent. The socialist is not looking for this happy event to take place in a world where there is life after death, but in the present material world in which we live. Socialism has no place for "pie in the sky some day by and by." It's all in the here and now. This flows out of the supposition that there is no life after death, nor is there any final cosmic judgment. The whole socialist scenario, according to

Marxism-Leninism, is guaranteed by science, which replaces God.

The creed of the socialists has a dogmatic basis even though it denies the existence of a divine being. As long as the socialist faithful believe the creed, the system has strength. When any creed is questioned by the faithful it is a sure sign that it is already losing its hold on them and points to grave trouble. At this moment in history there is only scant evidence to show that the socialist creed by and large is in the process of being undermined by criticism among the faithful.

There are only two ways by which a creed can be effective or determine the destinies of people. The first is when the people have an inward conviction of the truth of the creed and of the cause it represents. The creed may not be true, but even the untrue can be a potent force if it is believed and held to strongly and without reservation by the people who work under it. The second way a creed can be made effective is by the use of raw power at the point of a gun. A creed which depends on the use of force for its continuance is on the downward path. But so long as the power which supports the creed is sufficient there is little hope for a change. In this regard socialism represents a peculiar picture. In some places it appears to be supported by faith in its theorums. In other places it is definitely supported by police power. There can be no question that the smaller European nations under the dominion of the Soviet Union (Poland, Hungary, Czechoslovakia, etc.) are socialist by compulsion, not by conviction. The absence of heart conviction in the credo of socialism leaves the Soviet Union with only two options. It can let the captive nations decide their own destiny and choose for or against socialism. Or the Soviet Union must resort to force to continue its dominion over smaller nations, which surely would falter in their attachment to socialism if free to determine their own destiny.

THE HUMAN NEED FOR
ETHICAL AND MORAL STANDARDS

Any religion or any system in which people congregate and act as a community must have some kind of ethical and moral standards normative for that society. What kind of system this constitutes, what its component elements consist in, and on what foundation the system rests are important. If there is no explicit articulation of the principles of conduct in the form of commandments such as the Mosaic Law, one can still determine what the principles are by looking at what the people of the community do.

The socialists have declared a state of war against free enterprise society. This fact in itself suggests the need to argue that a free enterprise economy is defective, that is, sinful, and runs counter to some morality. Socialism also says that when it can happen no other way, violence is the last resort by which free enterprise will be overthrown. What form violence takes is immaterial, for any means which will bring about the demise of free enterprise is looked upon as acceptable.

It was Lenin who pronounced the dictum that the criterion of right action is the degree to which it helps and promotes the cause of the revolution to overthrow free enterprise. Using this premise, the Soviet Union has practiced deception, lying, and treachery. It has been characterized by ruthlessness, contempt for fair play, and a complete disregard for the notion that the means to an end must be proper. This nation has been completely dishonest by its perversion of facts, and by the fabrication of or the distortion of facts.

The day-to-day conduct of the socialists, whether it be that of the Soviet Union, Cuba, the Peoples' Republic of China, or any other socialist state, raises the question whether socialism has an ethic and a morality and what it is if it does. Marxism is Hegelian in its philosophic orientation. The dialectic of Hegel denies that there are any absolutes—eternal and immutable principles on which to base a system of ethics and morality. It was easy, therefore, for Karl Marx to say that ethics is part of the superstructure created by the conditions of production. Translated into simple terms it means that all morality and ethics are class related. Since bourgeois society is in control at this moment and the proletariat waits for its liberation from its domination at the hands of the bourgeoisie, the present system of ethics and morality is that of the bourgeoisie. Thus ethics and morality are relative, not absolute.

It is no accident that *The Communist Manifesto* says nothing about *right* or *justice*. Yet from the propaganda perspective the pejorative words, *wrong* and *unjust*, are consistently applied to free enterprise. Marx himself in *Das Kapital* everywhere reveals his total abhorrence of free enterprise. He persistently argues that it is inherently corrupt. This leaves open the question of how it can be so, if there are no standards against which it can be tested. If free enterprise is truly evil, it must be contrary to some objective moral principle which enables one to pronounce definitive judgment. But the socialists deny the existence of any such principle.

SOCIALIST ETHICS AND MORALITY

Two statements, one by Engels and the other by Lenin, reveal what the socialist viewpoint is on ethics and morality. The first is from the pen of Engels:

We therefore reject every attempt to impose on us any moral dogma whatsoever as an eternal, ultimate, and forever immutable moral law on the pretext that the moral world too has its permanent principles which transcend history and the differences between nations. We maintain on the contrary that all former moral theories are the product, in the last analysis, of the economic stage which society has reached at that particular epoch. And as society has hitherto moved in class antagonisms, morality was always a class morality; it has either justified the domination and the interests of the ruling class, or, as soon as the oppressed class has become powerful enough, it has represented the revolt against this domination and the future interests of the oppressed. That in this process there has on the whole been progress in morality, as in all other branches of human knowledge, cannot be doubted. But we have not yet passed beyond class morality. A really human morality which transcends class antagonisms and their legacies in thought becomes possible only at a stage of society which has not only overcome class contradictions but has even forgotten them in practical life (R. N. Carew Hunt, *The Theory and Practice of Communism*, NY: Macmillan, 1954, pp. 78, 79).

Lenin, the heir of Marx and Engels, had this to say:

Is there such a thing as Communist ethics? Is there such a thing as Communist morality? Of course there is. It is often made to appear that we have no ethics of our own; and very often the bourgeoisie accuse us Communists of repudiating all ethics. This is the methods of throwing dust in the eyes of the workers and peasants.

In what sense do we repudiate ethics and morality?

In the sense that it is preached by the bourgeoisie, who derived ethics from God's commandments. . . . Or instead of deriving ethics from the commandments of God, they derived them from idealist or semi-idealist phrases, which always amounted to something very similar to God's commandments. We repudiate all morality derived from non-human and non-class concepts. We say that it is a deception, a fraud in the interests of the landlords and capitalists. We say that our morality is

entirely subordinated to the interests of the class strug-
gle of the proletariat. Our morality is derived from the
interests of the class struggle of the proletariat. . . . The
class struggle is still continuing. . . . We subordinate our
Communist morality to this task. We say: Morality is
what serves to destroy the old exploiting society and to
unite all the toilers around the proletariat, which is
creating a new Communist society. . . . We do not believe
in an eternal morality (ibid., pp. 79, 80).

Lenin was so opposed to religion, Jewish, Christian, or otherwise, that he exclaimed: ". . . every religious idea, every idea of god, even every flirtation with the idea of god, is unutterable vileness." He also said, "Any person who engages in god-building, disparages himself in the worst possible fashion." If all of this is true then any religion which has room for a god of any kind is impossible in Marxist thinking. The irony of Lenin's bitter attack against theism lies in the fact that only one who is himself omniscient could make such statements. And whoever is omniscient is, of necessity, God. So Lenin, in making such statements, is subconsciously proclaiming himself to be God and is thus a theist. In other words, his statements prove the very point he labored to destroy.

From the statements of the founding fathers of the socialist enterprise, we may conclude that their ethical system is materialistic and naturalistic. The familiar phrase "the concrete human situation" which rejects every transcendent element is the foundation stone for the socialist ethic. It rejects any objective standard applicable at all times under which men should function. Once the presuppositions of the socialists are accepted, then certain conclusions are apparent:

1. Nothing is final or sacred. Everything is in a state of flux. All morality is relative to class interests. Every class has its own morality.

2. Since everything is in a state of flux, there can be no

enduring standard of right and wrong for all times.

3. Progression in history becomes the standard for judgment. Whatever points "forward" is the equivalent of good. Whatever points "backward" is the equivalent of bad. Struggle is the substitute for intrinsic excellence in conduct.

4. Ethics and morality must be subordinated to the interests of the class struggle. Anything which will bring about the defeat of the bourgeoisie and the victory of the proletariat is justified. That is, the end justifies the means; anything goes.

5. It is impossible to say that truth and love are better than falsehood and malice.

6. Marxism must reject the Judeo-Christian tradition, for its acceptance would entail pronouncing adverse judgment on Marx himself and the whole system.

7. Marxism's judgment against capitalism (that is, free enterprise and the bourgeoisie) is irrational and internally contradictory. Why? The theory of the class struggle requires that the bourgeoisie are bound to be what they are and to act as they do. Since there are no eternal moral and ethical standards, how can Marxism condemn the bourgeoisie (capitalists, or free enterprisers) who are what they are by nature and who cannot help themselves? No one can be morally indignant against anyone else's actions unless there is an enduring standard by which to judge one's conduct. But if no one is free to act contrary to his class morality, how can he be judged faulty unless the proletariat viewpoint is normative? The Marxist says, however, that there is no normative morality. Thus the Marxist case falls to the ground.

When Ronald Reagan became President of the United States one of the first statements he made about the Marxists was directed to the chief of them all, the Soviet Union. He said that "its leaders reserve 'the right to commit any crime, to lie, to cheat' in seeking 'world revolution.' " Some people professed to be shocked by the statement. Certainly it was bald enough. The only correct question was whether Mr. Reagan was stating the case fairly and in accord with Marxist teachings. Indeed Mr. Reagan was right on target. If it offended anyone, then his offense was telling the truth. Since socialist ethics endorses as right anything that furthers the cause of their endeavors, lying, cheating, stealing, murder, assassinations, and envy are appropriate.

Mr. Reagan's statement was based upon an entirely different approach to the matter of ethics. He was speaking from the Judeo-Christian perspective. He was saying that these things are wrong and no one has the right to use them for any reason. Moreover, he was not speaking as though these prohibitions are part of bourgeois morality. Rather he was saying that they are of the essence of life and must govern human relationships for all time. If there was a weakness in the Reagan approach it was this: A nation's walk must live up to its talk. The unfortunate fact is that in the United States public and private morality do not always conform to this dictum. The nation and its people do not always practice what they preach. But at least they claim to support a value system in agreement with the Judeo-Christian tradition.

When Mr. Reagan took the oath of office he agreed to protect and defend the constitution of the United States and the nation itself against all enemies domestic and foreign. But if this oath is not genuine it means nothing. The slogan found on the currency of the United States, "In God We Trust," is another illustration of its value system. Every court requires of witnesses a promise to tell the truth, the whole truth, and nothing but the truth. This is another illustration of the ethical standards of the nation.

When presidents lie to the nation, as Mr. Nixon did about Watergate, and when politicians steal from the people, pervert their office by taking bribes, and commit other crimes, they are doing what the socialists accept in principle and apply in practice. The socialists must be acknowledged as consistent. They practice what they preach. Whereas in the United States all too many, including those who mouth allegiance to free enterprise, do not practice what they profess to accept in principle. To be a hypocrite one must practice the opposite of what he claims to believe. The socialists, however evil they are, are not hypocrites. They do exactly what they say they will do and hold to a system of ethics which they use all the time. Nations like the United States and its people are the true hypocrites whenever they do what they condemn in others.

A word must be said about corporations and their private and public morality. These represent free enterprise and are large enough to have visibility before the public. Corporations can be and some are either amoral or immoral. Corporate decisions are made by individuals in the long run. They make these decisions behind the corporate shield. This allows for them to do what they would not do as individuals or even as church members. They function one way in their private lives and another in their roles in corporate structures. It is a split personality syndrome, for they sometimes do in corporate life what they would not do in private life. When corporations or even private businessmen fail to apply Judeo-Christian ethical precepts in their business lives they are not engaged in the kind of free enterprise based on the tradition of which we speak. In their practices they have fallen into the ethical system which underlies socialism.

Socialism is not amoral; it is immoral. Its very nature, that is, its basic philosophy, makes it that way. Its economic theory (no private ownership of the means of production), its repudiation of human rights, and its denial of all true freedoms, its use of force, and its totalitarianism are all indicators of its immorality. We must remember that there is no other form of socialism existent anywhere that is not Marxist. Sweden and Britain, for example, are welfare states where there is some public ownership and some private ownership of the means of production. This mixture leans more and more toward full socialism. If and when it comes to power it will do exactly what Marxist socialist states always have done—take away freedom.

In a world filled with imperfect people there is no perfect society or economic system and there never will be. This fact does not mean there is no reason to prefer one system over another. Free enterprise (capitalism), despite the fallen nature of man, is distinctly preferable to socialism. As we have said and must say again and again, free enterprise will do a better job in meeting and improving the material conditions of men than socialism. The greatest danger to free enterprise is government intervention which interferes with the operation of the free market. Intervention keeps failing enterprises in business at the expense of the consumer, and it constitutes a hidden form of taxation which takes from the taxpayer money he could spend or save to improve the material condition of the nation and increase its wealth.

Free enterprise which has its roots in the Judeo-Christian tradition is likewise bound by the ethics of that system. If free enterprise employs in practice the system advocated by the socialists it is the surest guarantee that free enterprise will fail, just as surely as socialism is going to fail in the long run. A free market economy undergirded by the view that lying, cheating and stealing are permissible, will not and should not long endure. It then becomes dog-eat-dog as it refuses to honor neighbor love. Greed, rather than self-interest based on altruism, must prevail. The present secularist bent of the United States bodes ill for its future. Secularism has its roots in the Enlightenment just as socialism does. Whatever viewpoint places man above God, and substitutes, as it must, its own world and life view, which is in opposition to the Judeo-Christian world and life view, must fail.

SOCIALIST ETHICS AND CLASS DISTINCTIONS

In all ages of men's history there has been a division of peoples into various classes. There has never been an egalitarian society in which all men were equal. There have always been the rulers and the ruled. The socialist system as we have noted previously operates on the assumption that there are only two classes of people—the bourgeoisie and the proletariat. Socialists emphatically and repeatedly attack the bourgeois class as the authors of every conceivable error. They go far beyond even this.

Socialists cultivate hatred between the two classes. They go even beyond hatred. They intend to destroy the bourgeoisie. And by this they do not mean they will wait until the bourgeoisie all die and hope they will be replaced by only the proletariat. They mean they will murder the bourgeoisie. The proclamation of Jesus in the Sermon on the Mount, "Blessed are the peacemakers for they shall be called the sons of God" is regarded as nonsense. More than that, it is looked upon as a device originated by the bourgeoisie to keep the proletariat shackled and bound in their chains. No socialist leader in any socialist state has ever tried to bridge the gap between the two classes they talk about. None has ever exalted the law of love or sought to bring understanding between the classes.

The outcome of socialist policy to rid the socialist state of these bourgeois parasites has been class genocide. This has been true whether it is the Soviet Union, the Peoples' Republic of China, Vietnam, or Cambodia. Multiplied millions of people have been brutally murdered and their murderers have boasted of what they have done. There never has been the slightest sign of remorse, nor has any Communist ever sought to repent for these atrocities. Let there be no illusion about the meaning of this ethic. The Communists encourage hatred against those nations which they call capitalist. Krushchev's statement that the Soviet Union intends to bury the "imperialists" (that is, the free enterprise people or capitalists) still stands.

It is true that the Soviets hope to take over the democracies without recourse to armed force. But once they accomplish this objective it will be but a short time before they eliminate whoever they regard as belonging to the bourgeois class. This intention signifies an ethic of hate, not of love. It is contrary to the teachings of virtually all religions and particularly that of the Judeo-Christian tradition. It is merciless, and it is so hardened that it will stop short of nothing to keep it from fulfilling its malign purposes.

What is chilling today is the fact that in places where the Christian faith has been a dominant factor in culture, there are so-called Christian ministers in the churches who call for the destruction of the free enterprise system. They do not seem to understand that there is no way that system can be destroyed without substituting a socialist totalitarianism in its place. Nor do they see that free enterprise cannot be extinguished by legislation or by force. In the long run these Marxist fellow travelers in the clergy who oppose capitalism will have to resort to the elimination of the bourgeoisie just as the Communists openly proclaim. Moreover, the abolition of free enterprise by these people must of necessity include their denial of the commandment against stealing, and the willingness to sacrifice the other human rights of which we have spoken, in order to keep free enterprise from rising amid the ashes of socialist inequities and inefficiency.

UTOPIAN SOCIALISM AND JUDEO-CHRISTIAN ETHICS

There are some utopian socialists of various kinds who claim some connection to the Judeo-Christian tradition. They are inconsistent when they do so. The same sort of inconsistency is apparent among the adherents of the theology of liberation who cover their Marxism with a thin veneer of Christianity. The World Council of Churches must be included in this medley of Christian socialists.

These socialists are deeply indebted to Karl Marx for his understanding of the historical process and they constantly mimic the phrase "the concrete human situation." They call upon the Old and New Testaments to pronounce their definitive judgment against free enterprise. At the same time they unhesitatingly act contrary to some of the basic teachings of the Testaments, which places them in a position of gross inconsistency. Almost without exception they advocate and support violence as the means to destroy free enterprise. They underwrite violence and lend financial support to it under the guise of medical and social help which is patently false. But even if these funds were so used it would simply release other funds which could then be redirected for armaments, guerrilla warfare, and terrorism.

The ethical errors of socialism are multiple. First the adherents violate the law of love by their approval of violence, terrorism, and the destruction of the bourgeoisie. Second, they violate the seventh commandment, "thou shalt not steal," when they approve of expropriating private property which inalienably belongs to others. Third, they violate the clearest teaching of the Old and New Testaments, as we have already shown, since the Testaments validate free enterprise, which the socialists reject.

These socialists fail to see that Marx took a position which was at least consistent—his acknowledgment that no form of socialism can be validated by an appeal to the Judeo-Christian tradition. The tough question is why advocates of socialism who profess adherence to the Judeo-Christian tradition, such as Gustavo Gutierrez, J. Miguez-Bonino, and Orlando Costas, do not see how correct Marx was. They should either reject socialism or the Judeo-Christian tradition.

It is especially difficult to see why these "Christian Marxists" who are supposedly acquainted with the Christian view of man fail to see that the faults in free enterprise are not intrinsic to the system itself. Rather the evils, when they appear, are easily traceable to the failure of men to practice what the Old and New Testaments command. These socialists should be working for the reformation of free enterprise, not for its destruction.

The selective use of the Old and New Testaments by socialists of this variety is characteristic. They accept what appeals to them and reject what they do not like. This ultimately undercuts their whole position, but it does not seem to have occurred to them. They fall into an epistemological dilemma that they have neither faced nor overcome. Once they have settled the question about the source of their authority they are bound to the use of all of it. Therefore when these "Christian socialists" reject parts of it and accept other parts, they have lost their authority. When they, rather than the Old and New Testaments, become the frame of reference, they have completely abandoned the Judeo-Christian tradition in principle. What is equally significant is that once they reject any part of their guidebook they bring into question those parts they choose to accept. And when what they choose to accept becomes the keystone of their viewpoint, they have elevated themselves above what they claim to be the source of their religious knowledge, and have effectively negated it in principle.

No one can be certain that these socialists are truly adherents of the Judeo-Christian tradition; they may be using it as a cover for what really is a commitment to straight Marxism. The best that can be said of them is that they are muddleheaded and unable to think Christianly. Meanwhile, they constitute a formidable threat both to free enterprise and to the Judeo-Christian tradition, a threat which must be accepted as such and responded to biblically and apologetically every step of the way. Their influence is such that many may be led astray by them and so cast their votes and their influence in favor of socialism.

ATHEISTIC EXISTENTIALISM AND ETHICS AND MORALITY

The atheistic existentialist entertains a far more reasonable viewpoint than either the Marxist socialist or the utopian socialist. Those who advocate this viewpoint argue that life is meaningless, that it does not make sense. They say there is no place for men in the universe. At best he is a cosmic accident. Jean Paul Sartre described what is the central thesis of this system of thought when he wrote:

Man can count on no one but himself; he is alone, abandoned on earth in the midst of his infinite responsibilities, without help, with no other aim than the one he sets for himself; with no other destiny than the one he forges for himself on this earth.

Once God is eliminated from the cosmos, it becomes a man-centered universe. Man is then the one point of reference. Sartre and others of this school of thought work their way through to the end to which Marxism logically leads. The atheistic existentialists have not been fooled by Karl Marx's naive optimism. Whereas Marx promised the attainment of an ideal society and proclaimed the perfectibility of man, the existentialist knows fully well that this is a pipe dream coming from a bowl loaded with opium, not from an understanding of real life. Once God is removed from the picture the very ground of man's being disappears. Eliminate God and man is also eliminated. Nothing makes any difference. And every system of ethics and morality gets mired down in the question, "From whence does man locate any authority to validate *any* system of ethics and morality?"

The atheistic existentialist has grasped what Marx failed to see and has carried the socialist dream to its logical conclusion, a conclusion which may be seen from what the socialists like to call "the concrete situation." Since men are alone, and determine their own destinies, the socialists at the top of the spectrum of the Soviet Union, Cuba, etc., have created for themselves a life situation in which they wield supreme political and social power and enjoy luxuries neither premiers nor presidents can approximate in the Western nations. Who has the chauffeur-driven limousines? Who has servants to cater to their every need? Who has the best food and wine? Who lives in the finest quarters, has the best Black Sea sands to bathe on, or the finest houses in the countryside? Who has the best medical care, the finest of the hospitals, and the best and fanciest shops where only the highest of the high can make purchases? These people enjoy the best of all possible worlds in the here and now, for there is no hereafter, no final judgment, and no God who demands an accounting of one's stewardship.

Hedrick Smith in his book *Russia*, written some years following his stay in the Soviet Union as a reporter for the *New York Times*, has portrayed the situation there with clarity and precision. The Soviet elite suffer from no illusions. They know their system does not work. They hold the people in bondage and allow for no dissent, no freedom of any kind which is worth the name. They enjoy their perquisites and neither by intention nor example do they present to the average Russian a portrait of those who have given up everything for the motherland or for the socialist cause. Rather they have reaped all the benefits at the expense of the common man.

What may be said about the straight socialists may

also be said about the utopian socialists who also fail to see the accuracy of the conclusions of the atheistic existentialists once God and the Judeo-Christian tradition are scrapped. Friedrich Engels was a wealthy bourgeois who never gave up his wealth for the socialist cause. He lived and died enjoying a life style common to the wealthy manufacturers of his day. And he used the profits from his wealth to provide for the maintenance of Karl Marx, who built his arguments against the bourgeoisie with money which was of bourgeois origin. Sidney and Beatrice Webb, utopian socialists, spent their lives in relative affluence while they tooted the socialist horn. Their income was derived from money which had come from the free enterprise system. In all of these cases socialism was not promoted by the proletariat but by those who were openly identified with the rich bourgeoisie, with this difference: They advocated the elimination of the bourgeoisie, but they were talking about all other bourgeoisie than themselves.

THE IMPLICATIONS OF SOCIALIST ETHICS

Socialism abhors human freedom of person, of speech, of movement, and of any criticism of the socialist system, as we have seen. It dehumanizes people by setting up a system which takes from all citizens the basic rights which belong to them by nature and by God. It sets up a judicial system designed to protect and perpetuate all manner of evils by use of the grossest methods of imprisonment, of drugs and confinement to mental institutions, and of death itself. No one has more accurately used words to paint a picture than Aleksandr Solzhenitsyn in his *Gulag Archepelago*. In it he makes known the awful brutality, the injustice, and the arrogant disregard of human values and especially the law of love. In *Cancer Ward* and *One Day in the Life of Ivan Denisovitch* one gets a glimpse of the horrors of a system which promises so much and delivers so little. Any system which is required to do what the socialist system must do in order to bring into being the ideal society bespeaks a purgatory which makes the ultimate objective far-fetched and raises a question: How can any good come out of so much evil? The answer is: It can't!

The natural outcome of socialist ethics can be seen in the way socialists act. In 1955 the United States 84th Congress in its first session published Document 85 titled *Soviet Political Treaties and Violations*. Almost without exception the Soviet Union has violated every treaty it ever made. Its performance has been so bad that no one in his right mind would sign a treaty with that nation expecting that the treaty would be kept. This leaves open the question of why any nation would be willing to sign a treaty unless there was attached to it such a significant and collectible penalty that the Soviet Union would find it impractical to break the agreement.

The Patent Office in the United States guarantees the right of the patent holder to receive royalties for the use of his invention by others. But copies of patents can be bought by anyone for a nominal sum. The Soviet Union buys copies of all patents and uses whatever it pleases without paying for the use of the inventions. It also publishes any books it chooses without paying royalties to the authors.

Socialism spreads its lies through every possible medium. Disinformation, which is deliberately intended to deceive, is used unceasingly. Lies known to be without foundation are supported by spurious evidences to give them a semblance of truth. Such distortions are not accidental. They are part of the apparatus used by the Soviets to destroy their opposition internally and externally.

In the case of Eleanor Roosevelt the Soviets constructed Potemkin Village as an illustration of how wonderful socialism was under the iron heel of Stalin. She was taken in by this showpiece, for the Soviets did not allow her to see other towns and cities which would have given her a far different picture of what real life was like under the totalitarian regime. She came home raving about the success of socialism and professed to see in it the wave of the future. Even today visitors can only go where the KGB wants them to go and they are under careful supervision most of the time. Tour guides direct visitors only to what their hosts wish them to see. And hotel rooms are bugged.

Communist newspapers in the United States and elsewhere hew to the socialist line and publish only what Moscow wants printed. The net result is sheer propaganda untouched by truth or reality. How bad the situation is can be seen from the use of terms which deceive readers who do not understand the Soviet doubletalk. Years ago the Canadian Intelligence Service listed some of the Aesopian language of the socialists and gave the true definitions of the terms. Thus a non-communist is a reactionary; an anti-communist is a fascist; bosses are employers; a warmonger is anyone strongly opposed to communism and who doesn't think their designs are honorable or that their demands should be met; cold war is resistance to communist policy; aggression is firm action used to prevent or defeat communist aggression; colonialism is possessing territory the communists want; slander is any exposure of communist aims, tactics, or techniques; inquisition is any legitimate inquiry into communist subversion or infiltration; a stool pigeon is an anti-communist worker; a McCarthyite is anyone who wants or suggests an investigation of communist subversion and espionage; peace is nonopposition to communism; peace lovers are those who support communism; peaceful coexistence is nonresistance to communist policy and revolutionary takeover; people's democracy is the communist slave state; an intellectual is a rich communist; eminent clergymen are those who follow the socialist line; famous lawyer is the term used for those who support communism and defend communists; a famous actor is anyone in Hollywood who is a communist; oppressed people are those living in the countries the communists wish to seize. This list could be enlarged many times. It is illustrative of the ethical and moral attitudes of the socialists.

Surely it should be apparent to any objective observer of the socialist system around the world that socialist ethics lie at the root of the problem. Some twenty years ago Fred P. Corson, then President of the World Methodist Conference, and a bishop of the Methodist Church said that communism is not moral. He wrote:

Before making agreements with Russia, the free world must ask: "How good is Communism?" To date we seem to be answering this question in terms of its military strength, scientific invention, and mass education. These facts are but secondary. The main consideration is ethical. What character, what kind of personality the moral philosophy of Communism produces should determine the trustworthiness of Communism and our evaluation thereof. The Communists' standard of action reveals their measure of integrity and tells us with what we must deal. Chesterton once observed that when you rent a room to someone, the real question to ask is not where he works or how much money he has, but rather, what is his philosophy of life. The advice could apply to nations also.

The basic question then, whether Mr. Krushchev gives a watch to a worker, calls for universal disarmament, or speaks of peaceful competition in coexistence is first and always the philosophy to which he is completely committed. The concept of "this jolly old Nikita" [you can put in the name of any other Communist leader or group you wish to including Leonid Brezhnev, Aleksei Kosygin, Fidel Castro, Chairman Mao, or the Sandinistas of

Nicaragua] *dare not fool us about the real Krushchev. As Editor Ralph McGill of the* Atlanta Constitution *said, "Remember when Krushchev turns on the charm that he also heads a police state." Read Marx and Lenin alongside the current news releases. World revolution, world domination by any means, has been Krushchev's training school. He is committed to the very same tactics. Remember he vowed to bury our system of free enterprise. Remember that in advocating trade agreements, he is not embarrassed to repudiate a $2,600,000,000 indebtedness to the United States. Remember Communism's endorsement of slave labor that incarcerates even now at least 12 million in Russian labor camps alone. When you think of your children, remember Marx's concept of man as a producing animal. Don't ignore what Overstreet said and verified, that "during 40 years of existence the USSR has set a world's record for breaking pacts." Remember [Grigori] Zinoviev's words on treaty making which Communist leaders have never repudiated, "We are willing to sign an unfavorable peace because it would only mean that we should use the breathing space obtained to gather strength." Remember the non-aggression pact signed with Estonia, Latvia, and Lithuania, and what happened to all three in Russia's "Little-Red-Ridinghood" act. Remember the 50 out of 52 agreements with Korea which the Reds have flouted and broken.*

These facts are but several illustrations of Dr. John Bennett's conclusion in Christianity and Communism: *"The only ethical test they [Communists] recognize is whether or not it serves the Communist cause, which in turn bears out Lenin's principle that 'there is room in life only for those who are troubled by virtue.' " We dare not stake our whole future on Russia's present "good faith," nor pay in advance for some eventual delivery of goods. Russia favors a "negotiation in crisis" strategy: Point one, create a crisis; point two, make demands;*

*point three, offer to negotiate. The result? A compromise in Russia's favor. By agreement we surrender what is ours; by agreement they get what was never theirs. With such strategy nothing ever gets properly nor finally settled. Reopened hostilities are a constant threat under such "blackmail" conditions. Take the Berlin situation, for example. Establishing peace is not Communism's chief concern. Rather, Communists want to maneuver themselves into a position where, if necessary, they can wage a successful war to gain control of Berlin. Conferences, therefore, either go on endlessly or end in stale-*mate ("Facing the Communist Menace," *Christianity Today*, April 27, 1962, pp. 716-719).

Two decades have passed since Bishop Corson wrote those words. The United Methodist Church of which Dr. Corson was a bishop has built up a splendid record of full support for the Soviet Union and all it stands for since his day. It has damned capitalism and proclaimed the glories of socialism. It has consistently denigrated non-communist nations like South Korea, South Africa, and the governments of Central American nations such as Nicaragua, El Salvador, and others before they were overtaken by communist revolutions. Bishop Corson's views are not typical of those of the leaders of the United Methodist Church today. Does this mean that the communist threat has disappeared? Was Bishop Corson wrong in his diagnosis? Has the lion become a lamb? Are the ethical principles of socialists really equal to or better than those of the Bible? The record of the socialists since 1962, when Bishop Corson wrote his article, is worse than anything he envisaged at that time. *America's Future* in its January 23, 1981, issue has this to say about the ethical operations of the communists in Latin America.

One of the gravest foreign affairs crises confronting the Reagan administration is the rapidly developing Soviet and Cuban threat in Central America and the Caribbean. Although the new administration intends to end Washington's policy of appeasing and accommodating leftist revolutionaries, the hour appears late for any effective U.S. action to stem the Communist tide now rolling toward our southern doorstep.

Even before President Reagan assumed office on January 20th, disgruntled U.S. Liberals were complaining that his election had encouraged diehard rightwing reactionaries to mount a renewed wave of "oppression" in Latin America. In reality, Moscow and Havana appear determined to push their guerrilla forces as fast and as far as possible before the United States can devise means of countering the Communists and helping the beleaguered non-Communists.

The urgency of the crisis is dramatized in a graphic and shocking new documentary film, "Attack on the Americas!" produced by the American Security Council. It opens with scenes of violence in war-torn El Salvador and elsewhere in Central America. "Today," says the narrator, "it is being invaded by those who march to a Communist beat. They speak of liberation and human rights. Their weapons are terrorism, sabotage, and assassination. The strategy comes from Moscow."

A triumphant Fidel Castro is shown addressing a rally of victorious Sandinista revolutionaries in Nicaragua last July. "For almost twenty years," the narrator continues, "Cuba was the solitary outpost of Communism in the Western Hemisphere. Today, Fidel Castro is exporting revolution throughout Central America and the Caribbean, waging 'wars of liberation' for his Soviet sponsors. But, this time the challenge is not half way around the world in Afghanistan or Southeast Asia, but in our own backyard."

In a series of interviews with leading defense and intelligence experts, "Attack on the Americas!" illustrates just how Castro and the Soviets are pursuing their

*strategic objective of "slashing the Americas in half" by
conquering the narrow land bridge separating the
United States and South America.*

*Lieut. General Gordon Sumner, Jr., former chairman
of the Inter-American Defense Board, warns that "the
Soviet is out to get at the United States by moving into
the socially, economically and politically troubled areas
of Latin America and to use them as a base of operations
against the United States."*

*The documentary reveals little known facts concern-
ing the critical importance of the Caribbean to U.S. oil
imports: "Fifty-six percent of our imported oil is refined
in this area. But it is the oil which passes through the
Caribbean from the Persian Gulf, Alaska, Nigeria and
Venezuela which makes this area one of vital interest to
Soviet strategists."*

Thus we can see the ethical standards of communism
which cares nothing for peace, human rights, and the
lives and material interests of the people of the
Americas. As if this were not enough, the same issue of
America's Future tells of "Soviet Secret Stealers."

*The Russians are resorting to some devious new schemes
to get around a U.S. ban on high technology exports to
the Soviet Union. Trade and intelligence experts report
that the Soviets are now using more and more third parties to obtain the technology needed to continue their
massive military buildup.*

*Ironically, one of the schemes involves the U.S. Free-
dom of Information Act under which large volumes of
government data, much of it previously classified, are
made available on request. There is evidence that many
of the requests originate with Soviet and Soviet-bloc
agents. Through American contacts, they ask for and
receive from federal agencies a wide variety of detailed
scientific and industrial information, including pat-*

ents, manufacturing methods and engineering designs.

One of the newest and cleverest Soviet techniques of obtaining U.S. technology involves third-party purchase of stock in U.S. companies. According to Pentagon sources, there are now more than 25 such American companies with Soviet-bloc shareholders. Most of these firms produce high-technology items, including advanced computers and electronics sought after by Moscow to fill vital gaps in its own technology. Informed sources in Washington say that a Pentagon attempt last summer to reveal the names of these companies was blocked by State Department officials who contended it would hurt detente.

The biggest loophole in the U.S. ban on technology to Russia is found in Western Europe. Despite routine attempts at export controls by an allied organization called COCOM—the Coordinating Committee—many NATO countries do little or nothing to prevent their bankers and traders from doing a brisk business in the export of both capital and technology to Russia and its satellites. On tap is a proposed $12 billion Soviet deal involving West German technology and a consortium of Belgian banks in the construction of a natural gas pipeline from Siberia to Western Europe. Payment would be in the form of Russian gas. West Germany, for example, would eventually depend on the Soviet pipeline for one-third of its natural gas needs.

Writing on "The Great Technology Giveaway" in the Washington Star, *investigative reporters Arnaud de Borchgrave and Michael Ledeen insist that even if the Reagan administration tightens export controls as part of a "linkage" policy aimed at curbing Soviet adventurism, it won't work without full cooperation by all of the allies.*

"For nearly two decades," they warn, "the West has been financing two separate defense budgets—its own, and a steadily increasing part of the Soviet bloc's."

These statements point up two facts: The first is that the Communists of all countries are devious and operate on an ethical wavelength far removed from any enduring standards, a system designed only to accomplish communist objectives by all possible means, however foul and outrageous. The second is that the nations of the West are assisting the Soviets in their designs and in effect are giving them the rope by which the Soviets will hang them once they gain control.

SUMMATION

We have come to the point where two opposing systems of ethics and morality can be looked at and a decision arrived at as to which system is superior to the other. When this is done it will be seen that the socialist ethical and moral system is wholly unacceptable, whether considered from the vantage-point of the Judeo-Christian tradition or from a purely rational one. The latter is based on that which best enables a culture to survive and to improve the material and spiritual conditions of mankind.

A few examples will illustrate what is involved in making a decision. Let us remember that the Judeo-Christian faith and religions generally teach that we are to do unto others what we would have them do to us. Or as Confucius stated it: We are not to do unto others what we would not want others to do to us. He was not saying this because he was an adherent of the Judeo-Christian tradition. He came to it from the Tao, that is, the sum of knowledge which is obvious to thinking people everywhere. Socialism denies this principle. Once the principle is denied, no one can have peace or confidence in his or her relationships with one another. A wife could not trust her husband nor could a husband trust his wife Children could not trust parents and vice versa.

The same situation exists with regard to the Mosaic

commandment about telling the truth—that is, the prohibition against lying. What kind of a human relationship can exist if it is known that lying is an acceptable practice? Once lying is accepted as an ethical standard, every relationship of life is emptied of meaning. If I never can be sure whether my wife is telling me the truth, there is no real basis for my marriage. From a psychological as well as from a practical standpoint, no one in his right mind would want a society based on lying. It may also be said that a free enterprise system based on lying would not work anymore than a socialist system based on it. It is difficult if not impossible to contemplate what a society would be like if all people in it were liars.

The Mosaic Law forbids stealing. If that commandment is of no value and if stealing is legitimated, the consequences are devastating. I would have to live in a fortress to protect myself against those who would seize my goods. I could not even be sure that my own wife and children might not steal them too. Nor could I have any confidence they would not take them and sell or trade them to others for reasons of their own.

So gross are the results of holding to a system of ethics and morality totally void of positive absolutes, that it is difficult for most people to understand the socialist mindset. When dealing with them, whoever assumes they operate on the same plane of thinking as do adherents of the Mosaic Law is sadly mistaken. To assume they will tell the truth, they won't steal, and they will do to others what others do to them is a wrong assumption. They will lie, cheat, and steal. They will break their agreements. They do look on those who accept such Judeo-Christian absolutes as idiotic and simpleminded. They will use their own system of ethics to accomplish their malign purposes, and demand at the same time that the non-communists adhere to Judeo-Christian principles, because the communists gain a distinct advantage when they do. In facing the communist menace, to dilute or abdicate a system of values which forbids lying, cheating, and stealing is no lasting solution. It would prove to be self-defeating. But this does not mean that there is no way to combat the ethical immorality of the communists. How can this be done?

The international community can act in concert by applying stringent rules governing the relations between the democracies and the socialist governments. The first principle is never to lend socialists money which you have no guarantee will be repaid. Second, sell nothing that is not paid for in advance in specie rather than rubles. Make no treaties with socialist states until they have shown from their right behavior that they have become trustworthy. And the moment they break any part of any treaty, disavow that treaty and make no more treaties. They are outcasts of society when they operate on the opposite basis to that of the democracies. Outcasts should be treated as just that. If the Western democracies who feed the Soviets were to demand gold or silver for their food and ship it only after the specie had been received, they could bring the Soviets to their knees in short order. If the Soviets used up their gold and silver for food they could not spend as much on armaments.

Whether it is a socialist nation or a Western democracy, no economic progress or expansion and improvement of the nation's material condition can come about without the use of capital. Capital can only come from somebody's savings, that is, what they do not consume. A large measure of socialist technocracy exists because Western technocratic nations have loaned the socialists capital to build their industrial enterprises. Right now it is estimated that the Soviets, for example, are deeply in debt to the Western nations for loans extended to them. The gravest mistake the democracies can make is to fund their announced enemies who publicly proclaim that they intend to bury them.

Free enterprise, in order to be free, rests on the pillars of trust and truthtelling. In this it stands in opposition to socialist ethics and morality. This brings home to men the decision which must be made between two systems which are opposed to each other: free enterprise controlled by an ethical system which stands opposed to lying, cheating, stealing, and which stands for neighbor love; the other is the socialist system based on the anti-Christian, anti-reasonable, and anti-human ethical and moral postulates which guarantee that a society so governed must fall apart and crumble in the dust.

Who in his right mind would choose the tyranny of socialism? Who would be naive or stupid enough to deprive himself of all he has to gain by refusing to place his confidence in free enterprise? The choice is really a choice between freedom and slavery, between statism and individualism, between some form of theism and atheism, between a view of man rooted in matter or man made in the image of his Creator, between democracy and totalitarianism, between that which is rational and that which is irrational, between the truth and the big lie, between the ethics of the Ten Commandments and the rootless relativities of Marxism, between a universe governed by law which gives man the necessary beneficent rules for life versus a mechanistic material view of life, based on matter without spirit. It is a choice between love and hate. It is as simple as that. And men are free to make their choice, not bound by a historical process which operates inexorably to bring to pass that which man can in no way alter or reverse. Granted the imponderables caused by the nature of man as a sinner, it should be clear to all that free enterprise controlled by the Judeo-Christian ethic is the only reasonable choice for men to make.

Our journey is over and the tale has been told. Whatever decisions are made between socialism and free enterprise will have lasting repercussions in the whole arena of life. Perhaps the wise words of some unknown scribe best sum up the theme of this work:

You cannot bring about prosperity by discouraging thrift. You cannot strengthen the weak by weakening the strong. You cannot help the wage earner by pulling down the wage payer. You cannot further the brotherhood of man by encouraging class hatred. You cannot keep out of trouble by spending more than you earn. You cannot build character and courage by taking away man's initiative and independence. You cannot help men permanently by doing for them what they could and should do for themselves.